Shattered But Not Destroyed

A Mother's Journey from Heartbreak to Hope

SHIRLEY H. SCARBOROUGH

ceopublishing
ILLUMINATING CREATIVITY

RICHMOND, VA

Shattered But Not Destroyed

This book is designed to create an immersive reader experience. Throughout this book, you will find the usage of QR Codes which will allow you to scan with the option of listening and viewing.

Look for this icon:

Visit us on the web! www.cryloudspeakup.com

ISBN: 978-1-964455-04-4 *Paperback*
ISBN: 978-1-964455-05-1 *Hardback*
ISBN: 978-1-964455-06-8 *E-Book*

This book is dedicated to the memory of my beautiful daughter, Francesca Harris-Scarborough. I am grateful for the precious years of memories we shared and for the love and joy that completed my life.

Though she is no longer here, my love for her will always endure. Forever etched in my heart.

CHAPTER
Contents

CERTAINTY IN MY UNCERTAINTY | *1*

SHATTERED | THE CALL THAT CHANGED MY LIFE | *8*

DEATH | THE NON-NEGOTIABLE | *17*

THE FINAL GOODBYE | *24*

A MOTHER'S LOVE | *37*

GRIEF | THE UNINVITED GUEST | *49*

KISSING FROGS | THE ILLUSIONS AND LIES | *61*

LOVE IS BLIND | IGNORING RED FLAGS | *67*

LONGING FOR LOVE | HER SILENT STRUGGLE | *78*

UNSPOKEN WORDS | THERE'S GOOD IN GOODBYE | *92*

A MOTHER'S CRY | TURNING PAIN INTO POWER | *99*

IS THERE A FRANCESCA IN YOUR HOME? | *109*

FORGIVENESS | MY PERSONAL STORY | *113*

DEAR YOU | *118*

SHATTERED BUT NOT DESTROYED

FOREWORD

LOVE . . . The Greatest Gift of All. Love is the purest and most profound gift, flowing freely from one heart to another. It is unbreakable, untouched by corruption, and divinely ordained. As Scripture reminds us in Matthew 22:39 [NIV], "Love your neighbor as yourself," and in John 13:34 [NIV], "A new command I give you: Love one another. As I have loved you, so you must love one another."

True love does not cause harm, nor does it seek to control or instill fear. Instead, love uplifts, conquering hatred and darkness. It shines not in words alone, but through actions. To love others deeply, one must first love and value themselves. Love cradles the heart, comforts the soul, and is demonstrated through the courage to walk away from anything that masquerades as love but brings pain. As the song reminds us, "Learning to love yourself is the greatest love of all."

Ms. Shirley took on the extraordinary challenge of raising her niece, whom she later adopted. Daily walking in love each day to provide her with the strength and tools to face adversity. Ms. Shirley's journey of love was not without its trials, but her commitment never wavered. Through it all, her steadfast love became a testimony—not only to her family but to the world.

It has been a privilege to bear witness to Ms. Shirley's story and the love that radiates through her life. It is my honor to share these words, inspired by her unwavering example of what it means to truly love.

With fondness and respect,
Carolyn Jones, Former Social Worker
Henrico County Department of Social Services

FOREWORD

It is indeed a divinely orchestrated privilege to write the foreword for this very revelatory and profound book, *Shattered but Not Destroyed: A Mother's Journey from Heartbreak to Hope,* but not just any mother, my beloved mother from Heartbreak to Hope. This is not just a book—it is a testimony, a lifeline, and a call to reflection for anyone who has ever walked through the valley of grief or struggled to find hope amidst despair.

As a pastor, I have often witnessed the dilemma of suffering in the lives of those I serve. The question, "Where is God in my pain?" and if God is real how could such a good God allow such tragic events to befall me? These are some of the most haunting cries of the human heart. In these pages, my mother, Shirley Scarborough, addresses that cry with a depth of vulnerability and spiritual insight that can only come from walking this path herself. Her journey of losing my sister and her beloved daughter, Francesca, in such a tragic and senseless manner, and the years of grappling with grief, anger, and unanswered questions, is laid bare with a raw honesty that pierces the heart. Yet, woven throughout her pain is the undeniable thread of God's sustaining grace.

This book is more than an account of tragedy; it is a roadmap to understanding God's Sovereign hand of love using the most difficult and very ugly experiences of loss and evil to reveal the beauty that is hidden in the ashes of fiery trials. My mother, Shirley, does not shy away from the hard questions: How do we move forward when life shatters our dreams? How do we navigate anger, forgiveness, and faith when justice seems absent? How do we turn pain into purpose? Her reflections, grounded in Scripture and illuminated by her own spiritual growth, guide readers to see that even in our brokenness, God is at work.

In a world where clichés are prevalent like, "God won't put more on you than you can bear," this book is a life manual reminding us of one of the greatest revelations mankind can ever comprehend that is in 2 Corinthians 1:8 [EHV], "Brothers, we do not want you to be unaware of the trouble that happened to us in the province of Asia. We were burdened so greatly, so far beyond our ability to bear it, that we even gave up hope of living."

God indeed does put more on us than we can bear for the express purpose of revealing the multifaceted face of grace, love and purpose of God! A God and Father who sacrificed his son to invite us to know him in a fellowship of suffering which cannot be compared.

Whether you are a mother grieving an unimaginable loss, someone struggling to find hope after a difficult season, or a person seeking to deepen your faith, this book will meet you where you are. It will challenge you, comfort you, and remind you that our God specializes in bringing life out of death, light out of darkness, and beauty out of ashes.

Shirley's courage to share her story, her unwavering faith, and her commitment to turning her pain into a platform for healing and empowerment is a testament to the God she serves. As you read these pages, you will be encouraged to rest in the promises of His plan and trust Him even when you can't trace him.

It is my prayer that this book will not only bring healing to your heart but will also inspire you to walk boldly in the assurance that God's grace is sufficient, His love is unchanging, and His plans for you remain good. Encouraging every reader to know whatever happened in your life, no matter how bad it seems, did not catch God by surprise. He wrote your past, present, and future, and is the author and finisher of your faith. I've read the end of the book HIS-STORY says you win!

With faith and love,
Pastor Robert Scarborough III., Son
The Word Church International Ministries

ACKNOWLEDGEMENTS

First and foremost, I want to give all glory and honor to God, who has been my strength, my comfort, and my ever-present help in times of need. Without His grace and guidance, this book would not exist. Through the darkest days of my life, when grief and sorrow seemed unbearable, His love has been my anchor.

This book is in memory of my beloved daughter, Francesca Harris-Scarborough. Though she is no longer here physically, her spirit will forever live in my heart. Her strengths, struggles and her story have inspired this journey. I always told Francesca that she was a world-changer, and now her story will change the lives of many women. Her voice will be heard. Though it was silenced in this world, it will still be heard. Through these pages, she will cry aloud, and her legacy will echo in the hearts of those who need to hear her message. Francesca's life, her challenges, and her triumphs will continue to inspire others to find their own strength and courage. She will always be remembered as a beacon of resilience and hope.

To my wonderful caring husband, her father, thank you for your unwavering love and support through the most difficult moments of our lives. Your strength, patience and compassion have been a source of comfort and stability. You have stood beside me through the storms of grief offering a shoulder to lean on and a heart full of understanding. Many nights I watched you grieve, sitting on the side of the bed, shaking your head, not wanting to say what you were thinking, your silent tears broke my heart. Sometimes I had to remember that we both lost our daughter. You showed me the depth of your love for her. Your quiet tears and your steadfast presence spoke volumes about the fatherly love you carried for her. Even in your own sorrow, you made room to hold me up when I couldn't find the strength to stand. You are not only an incredible husband, but an extraordinary father, whose love and devotion have shaped our family. I am forever grateful to walk this path with you by my side, with my love forever.

To my son, thank you for guiding me spiritually and emotionally through some of the hardest moments of my life. Your wisdom, faith and love have been a powerful anchor for me, especially during the times when I felt overwhelmed by grief. Watching you grieve not only as a pastor and son but as Francesca's brother has been heartbreaking, yet humbling. Your strength in the face of such a personal loss has been incredible. I know losing your sister has been deeply painful and your ability to still lead, support and pray through it all speaks to your resilience and devotion. I am grateful for your prayers, counsel and unwavering support.

To my beautiful daughter, LaShara, and to her loving husband, Arek, I've seen your heart break in ways only a sister could understand. The bond between sisters is irreplaceable, and I know your grief runs deep. I know the loss has been heavy on your heart, and I've watched you mourn quietly, yet powerfully. Thank you both for your support, prayers and love.

To my beautiful grandchildren, each of you has brought so much light and joy into my life, even during the darkest times of grief. Sariyah and Kamari, your calls, hugs, kisses and compassion was just what the doctor would have ordered for me. I saw your strength and watched how deeply you grieved and was affected by your Aunt Franny's death. Though you're young, you've shown such understanding and empathy, and I am so proud of who each of you is becoming.

To Baby AJ, you are a God-send. Born 19 days before Francesca's death. Your presence has been like therapy for me. You are a reminder of life, love, and hope in the midst of sorrow. Your life brings healing and joy to me each day.

To my mother, Florence Burrell, and the memory of my late father, Lorenzo, I thank you both for being there for me. So many days, I would walk in your house and flood your room with tears. I remember my father-in-law just hugging me and say it's going to be alright. He would tell me God sees everything, and that justice would be done. My mother would say it's going to be alright lil' girl. Somehow their hugs and words made everything ok.

To my siblings, thank you for your prayers. Your support has been my source of strength and a lifeline during my dark times. On days when I didn't know what to do or how to go on, one of you would call, pray with me, or gently feed me the Word of God. I am so grateful for all of you.

To my sisters, Linda Pryor, Constance Lewis, Sarah Ward, Joan Boyd, thank you for praying, calling to check on me, and crying with me. Sometimes you didn't have words, but that was ok, your presence and tears spoke louder than words ever could. To my sister Jean, thank you for standing in the gap just like Mama used to. Your compassion and wisdom always came together when I needed it most. Sometimes, you cried more than I did, and I felt your love and prayer through those tears. Thank you. To my sisters Kendra Coles and Ruth Williams, thank you for checking on me and making sure I knew you were there.

To Rhonda Holloway, thank you so much for your prayers and support. Thank you for using your creative gifts, for loving Francesca and for your heart.

To my brothers Oliver, Lionel, and Marshall, thank you for being strong for me. Your prayers and love were felt every step of the way. A very special thanks to my brother Gregory for checking on me every day.

A special thank you to my nieces and nephews who also called and checked in on me. Jahmal and Tasha Harris, thank you for your prayers and support. Tara Winston, thank you for sticking with me through it all.

To Jonathan and Raishaun Minor, my extended family, thank you for all of your kindness, sacrifices, prayers, compassion, and love that you have so generously shown to me and my family. Rai, you stepped in during the worst time of my life, never allowing me to carry the burden alone. I am deeply grateful for the way you ministered not just to me but to my entire family, with such grace and compassion. Thank you for being my safe place and for not judging me.

Jonathan, thank you for being you, for always lightening the load. In the midst of my tears, you found ways to make me laugh. That is something I will never forget. I thank God for the ministry of love He has placed within you and how He's allowing you to share that love with us. You both were truly God sent, and I will always cherish you.

Tivoli Dabney, words could never express my gratitude to you for all that you have done and continue to do. I know God placed you in my life for such a time as this. I have gleaned so much from your wisdom and expertise in many areas. I am forever thankful. Thank you for being my sounding board. I would like to thank your kind and patient husband, Christopher Dabney for allowing you to help guide me through this book and in establishing *Cry Loud, Spare Not, Speak Up, Inc.*, our non- profit organization. May God bless you and grant you every desire of your heart. May your dreams and visions come to pass.

To my wonderful Word Church Family, words cannot express how deeply grateful I am for all your prayers and unseen acts of kindness that have carried me and my family from April 9, 2020 to the present day. The meals you prepared, the phone calls, and the blessings you've showered upon us have been a lifeline. Your love is truly indescribable. Thank you, Sis. Wanda Mclaughlin and the Intercessory Prayer team for praying when I had no words or strength. Thank you, Minister Jontille Ray, and the Real Armed Women of God for your loving arms, your kind words, for wiping my tears, and for standing by my side. Thank you, Minister Arthur Coles and the Mighty Men of Valor, for loving on my husband, helping him through, for every kind word or deed for our family. Thank you to every auxiliary minister, please know that if I wrote down every single person's name and act of kindness, this book would be as thick as a dictionary. Thank you to each and every person who has been a part of this journey. Thank you from the depth of my heart. You are a part of this story and your love has helped me to move forward.

To my Cry Loud team, thank you for your support, dedication, and love throughout this difficult journey. Your prayers, encouragement, and hard work have meant the world to me and have been a true testimony to what it means to stand together in faith and purpose. Your commitment to *Cry Loud, Spare Not, Speak Up, Inc.* has touched so many lives, and I am forever grateful for the way you have shared your time, and hearts, for your helping hands and prayers. Together we've built something special, an outlet for healing, change, and hope. From the bottom of my heart, thank you

Thank you to all my friends and everyone that spoke life when I felt as though I was in a dead place.

INTRODUCTION

In the quiet moments of our lives, we rarely anticipate the earth-shattering call that will forever change our world. We pride ourselves as mothers in protecting our children with our lives regardless the price. For many, our children become our purpose for existing. This book begins with such a call from the Richmond Police Department that broke my heart into pieces for my daughter, Francesca Harris-Scarborough. This was a moment that no parent should ever have to face, and it thrust me into depths of grief I could never have imagined.

Shattered But Not Destroyed is a deeply personal recounting not just of that terrible tragedy, but more importantly, what unfolded in its aftermath. This narrative explores the rollercoaster of emotions — the relentless waves of sorrow, the endless questions without answers, and the struggle to find a way forward. My journey was not just through the landscape of grief but towards unexpected strength and hope.

Throughout this journey as a mother, my faith in God became my anchor. Despite the oppressive grief and moments when my faith wavered, I clung to the promises of God, drawing strength from them to navigate the seemingly impossible. This book is a testament to that faith, illustrating how the will to persist and divine guidance can sustain us even through seemingly insurmountable challenges.

This work also serves as an urgent call to address the often-hidden epidemic of domestic violence. It depicts the characteristics, choices, and actions of those living in abusive relationships with unhealthy mindsets. By sharing my daughter Francesca's experiences along with her writings, I aim to shed light on the unspoken struggles many women face and their compromises for love. The book aims to educate on recognizing warning signs, promoting self-worth, and encouraging young women to break free from abusive relationships and a low self-worth, value, and small expectations in return.

In the wake of unimaginable loss, I discovered a resilience I didn't know I possessed. My choice was clear: to let grief consume me or to channel it into purpose. I chose the latter, dedicating myself to raising awareness about domestic violence and ensuring Francesca's struggles, identity, and loss is not in vain. This memoir shares practical steps on navigating through grief, finding one's identity beyond pain, and transforming despair into empowerment.

It also addresses the kryptonite of every relationship and healing, which is forgiveness. Forgiveness has been a critical, challenging part of my journey. It was not just about freeing myself from anger, but about understanding and trusting in God's greater plan. This section of the book provides insight into the healing power of forgiveness and how it can liberate us from our own prisons of bitterness.

Ultimately, this is a story for anyone who has faced loss, betrayal, or deep sorrow. It serves as hope for the parent who is watching their beloved child make bad decisions, while helplessly observing as their decisions unfold into painful consequences. It is a story of hope — of how we can find light even in the darkest moments, how being shattered does not equate to being destroyed, and how faith and resilience can help us rise again.

This book invites you to join me on a journey of healing and rediscovery, providing guidance and inspiration for anyone seeking to turn heartbreak into hope. You'll find practical strategies for recognizing unhealthy relationships, uncovering inner strength, and transitioning from grief to a renewed sense of purpose.

What You Will Discover:
- Learn to identify unhealthy patterns and the warning signs of domestic violence, increasing awareness and safety.
- Discover inner strength to tackle life's toughest challenges with courage and resilience.
- Overcome the unique challenges that arise from starting over amidst hardship.
- Distinguish between the dreams and realities of relationships for informed and healthy choices.
- Reclaim a sense of self and purpose following profound grief and begin anew.
- Use sorrow as a catalyst for positive change, helping and inspiring others.

- Embrace the healing power of forgiveness, freeing yourself from anger and bitterness.
- Find peace and growth even in the absence of clear answers.
- Gain guidance to assemble broken pieces and move forward with strength.
- Build strategies to thrive despite challenging beginnings.
- Journey through deep sorrow to a place of healing and renewed purpose.

In this compelling memoir, uncover a narrative that speaks to anyone who has lowered their standards while seeking to be loved and accepted, or seeking to recover from rough beginnings or deep pain. Know that you were created out of love. There is a God that will love you unconditionally and will guide every step of your life. He has mapped out your life with a future you never imagined. His love will never quit. Our struggle comes into play when we argue with His love internally leading to desperate actions for what He has already provided. You are loved, seen, and worthy of true transparent and exclusive love.

This book offers a message of hope, tactics for recovery, a channel of support, and relief through truth for mothers. Even when life shatters us, we can rise stronger, channeling our experiences into a force for good. Through faith, resilience, and love, we can find the path to healing and a brighter future. No matter how broken we may feel, we can rebuild and rise stronger than ever before.

CHAPTER
One

CERTAINTY IN MY UNCERTAINTY

SHATTERED BUT NOT DESTROYED

Dear Journal

"

Life is truly a roller coaster with ups and downs and highs and lows.

"

Francesca

1 *Chapter*

CERTAINTY IN MY UNCERTAINTY

Life is an unpredictable journey. It's filled with moments that can shift without warning, plunging us into the unknown.

From the moment I woke up on Thursday, April 9, 2020, there was an inexplicable sense of foreboding, as if the air itself was thick with a warning that something was amiss. The sky was a patchwork of clouds. It seemed as though there was a battle as to whether the sun would break out or if the day would descend into gloom. The chill in the air wasn't just a physical sensation; it seeped into my bones, a cold that resonated with unease I felt deep within. I couldn't quite put my finger on it, but something was off.

I had planned to wake up by 4:30 AM, lead the prayer line, get dressed and arrive at work by 6 AM, which was my usual routine. This routine had always brought a sense of order and predictability to my life, but not *this* day. Even after leading the prayer line, while driving to work, I felt an overwhelming need to continue with my praise and worship through music. But that day, I felt anxious and uneasy, instead of the peace that usually followed prayer.

When I arrived at my office, I closed the door behind me and prayed some more, feeling the weight of something unknown pressing on my spirit. After praying, I heard in my spirit the words, "I am your certainty in your uncertainty." The phrase struck me as strange, almost Shakespearean, but I knew it was important so I wrote it down. Later, I spoke to my son-in-law and shared with him what had been revealed to me in prayer. He asked if he could post it on Facebook and I agreed. God was confirming to me that I could trust him. Not a day that goes by that I neglect to ask God to have his way and to let his will be done in my life. Despite my best effort to maintain control, to go on about my day as usual, I was merely reminded that only God is in true control.

Isaiah 55:8-9 [NIV] says, *"For my thoughts are not your thoughts, neither are your ways my ways,"* declares the Lord. *"As the heavens are higher than the earth, so are my ways higher than your ways and my thoughts than your thoughts."* This verse reminded me that God's perspective is so much greater than mine that he sees the full picture while I only see a small part. His thoughts and ways are beyond my comprehension, but they are always driven by his love and his purpose.

Despite the overwhelming uncertainty, there was one thing I could be certain of – God's promises. I clung to the truth that he would never leave me, nor forsake me as he promises in his word. I didn't know what the future held, but I knew that God would be with me every moment, giving me strength to make it through the darkest days.

> ❝ No matter what you face in
> *life,* don't let go of *God's* hand. ❞
> UNKNOWN

Proverbs 16:9 [NLT] says, "*We can make our plans, but the Lord determines our steps.*"

We start each day with plans, expectations, and hope for the future. On April 9, 2020, out of nowhere, the phone rang and in an instant, my life changed. All my plans I had so carefully laid out for the day and my life were abruptly erased. That call shattered not only my daily routine but also my heart, leaving me in a place of sorrow and deep grief, struggling to comprehend this new reality.

In that moment my heart felt so empty and devastated beyond words. I wasn't sure if it could ever be put whole again. My eyes wept and so did my spirit. I was broken. But even in my brokenness, God began to gently meet me in my pain. Through prayer, the love of others, and his comforting presence, He reminded me that He was still with me, even when I couldn't feel Him. He didn't take the pain away instantly, but He gave me the strength to take one small step at a time, leading me to moments of healing and hope. Slowly, I began to realize that though my plans were shattered, His plans for me were still good, and His purpose was still unfolding. It was through this restoration that I found the courage to trust Him again and to believe that life could hold meaning, even after such loss.

I want to encourage and remind you that life goes on - even when it feels impossible. Our plans may be shaken, turned upside down in ways we would never have chosen, but God's plans for us remain steady, even when we don't understand it.

Jeremiah 29:11 [NIV] assures us, *"For I know the plans I have for you,"declares the Lord, plans to prosper you and not to harm you, plans to give you hope and a future."*

God's plans for us are filled with purpose and promise, even in the midst of pain. Though my journey has been marked by deep heartache, God has shown me that His strength within us is greater than any darkness we face, and that same strength is available to you, ready to carry you through your hardest days.

If anyone had told me that I would be writing a book about the death of my daughter, about grief, that was yet focused on the goodness of God, I wouldn't have believed it. Yet, through God's love, I have found purpose in the midst of great loss. I have learned that no matter what challenges life brings, God's love and plans for us remain unshaken.

REFLECTION |

What plans did you make concerning a situation and you have had to trust God in your uncertainty?

_____

_____

_____

_____

_____

_____

_____

_____

CHAPTER
Two

SHATTERED | THE CALL THAT CHANGED MY LIFE

SHATTERED BUT NOT DESTROYED

Dear Journal

> "
>
> I've cried my last tear. I'm done. I think I'll get some boxes and tape and pack up my heart, label it 'Fragile'.
>
> "

Francesca

2 Chapter

SHATTERED | THE CALL THAT CHANGED MY LIFE

That morning, after finishing my devotions, I started working on files, greeting clients, and talking with staff. Around 7:30 a.m. the phone rang, it was the Richmond Police Department. Even before the caller could introduce himself, just hearing the words, "Richmond Police Department" made my heart race, my mind flooded with questions. He introduced himself as Detective Larry, from the Crime Unit. Once again, I started questioning why he was calling me, I was hoping he had the wrong number until he asked if I was Shirley Scarborough. I answered sharply, "Yes, I am" He proceeded to ask me to meet in person, as he couldn't share the details over the phone. I told him I had not committed a crime and couldn't comprehend why he needed to meet with me. I didn't know anyone that had committed a crime either. He responded that he needed to speak with me in person. Reluctantly, I agreed to meet at 10:30 AM. I dreaded meeting with the detective. I didn't know why, but a deep fear gripped me as I started analyzing my life, making sure I hadn't unknowingly committed a crime. The detective informed me that my husband, Robert, needed to be present as well. This made the situation feel even more serious.

As we arrived home at 10:10 AM the first thing that caught my eye was a small card wedged into the front door. As we approached the door, I looked at the card and saw that it was from the crime unit, my heart began to race again, and a wave of uncertainty washed over me. Was this the meaning behind all of that morning's anxiety?

The sight of that card brought an overwhelming sense of fear. Many questions bombarded my mind, each one more terrifying than the last. What could be prompting this visit from the crime unit? Did something happen to a family member? Could it be one of my children?

I checked the time again, trying to make sense of it. It was something about that card that gnawed at my spirit, making me even more impatient. My

8

husband and I exchanged glances as it seemed to take the detectives forever. Robert eventually busied himself with his car, working under the hood. I nervously worked around the house, starting several tasks but completing none of them.

Finally, the doorbell rang. When I opened the door, two detectives stood there. They were both calm and professional. The somberness in their demeanor made my heart sink even more before they uttered a word. They both identified themselves. One spoke in a measured tone, introducing himself as a detective from the crime unit. Those words sent a cold shiver of fear down my spine.

I called for my husband to join us. As we sat together bracing ourselves for the worst, it seemed like moments stretched into eternity. The detective finally asked, "Do you know Francesca Harris-Scarborough?" My husband and I each replied the same answer in unison, "Yes, that's my daughter." I showed him a picture of her on the living room table and said, "that's her. I asked what's wrong with Franny? Is she ok?" In my heart, I knew something was terribly wrong. The next words he spoke shattered my heart into a million pieces. "I'm sorry," he said. Those two words shattered the little hope I was clinging to. "Your daughter was found dead in her car this morning. She was shot in the heart."

When I heard those words, it felt as though the world around me had collapsed. I remember crying out loud, my voice echoing through the room like that of a child overwhelmed by unbearable pain. It was a raw primal reaction; a sound that came from the deepest part of me, where my worst fears had been buried. I lost it. Everything became fuzzy. My body went numb, as if my mind was trying to protect me from the full impact of the words. Yet at the same time, a searing pain cut through the numbness, a pain so deep and profound that it threatened to consume me. The detective's next words became distant, almost like background noise. I tried my best to process, to digest the devastating news. He spoke with kindness and compassion and was very apologetic, but there was no softening the blow. It was as though the news had deeply affected him as well. I felt lost, and uncertain of what to do next. My husband and I clung to each other, trying to establish some stability in our world that had been just shattered beyond recognition.

I laid in my husband's arms. His grip was tight, almost as if he was holding him on for dear life, trying to anchor himself in the midst of this tragedy. We didn't speak. There were just no words to say. As I looked at my husband's face, I saw shock and disbelief. The tears welled up in his eyes and yet he was trying to stay strong for me. We had lost our daughter. I wanted to see her. I needed to see her. I needed to make sure it was her. I was hoping this was a mistake. The Detective told me that they had positive identification, and I couldn't see her. At that point the medical examiner had her. He later explained that I wouldn't have wanted to see her like that. He said that she had been shot twice in the heart. He added that Franny had been murdered the night before, around 9:00 PM, which meant she was in her car until she was found at 6:30 the next morning.

My mind was in a state of shock. This couldn't happen to me or my family. This is something you hear on the news. One of the stories that catches your attention because someone's lost their life. You're sorry for the family, but your life continues on because it didn't affect your household. This was traumatizing, because it paralyzed my day, my plans and my future. Then, I understood why I couldn't shake off the feeling after praying that morning.

Psalm 46:1 [NIV] says, "God is our refuge and strength, an ever-present help in trouble". The reality of what we had just heard was too horrific to process. That day my cries were not just for my loss, but for the loss of the life that was so cruelly ripped away. The tears I cried on that day, on yesterday, as I'm crying as I write this story today, and the ones I will cry tomorrow, are a testament to the love I have for my daughter and the indescribable agony of losing her.

> **❝ And on that day it was then that I learned what a *broken heart* truly felt like. ❞**
> UNKNOWN

That day, I thought my plans, dreams and future were shattered with my heart. The pain was nothing like I had ever known, an ache so deep, it felt as though my soul was splintered into pieces. I was in a horrible pit of devastation.

As I reflect on the state I was in, my heart is truly grateful and thankful to God.

I want to encourage you, though the pain may feel overwhelming right now, know that healing is on the way. Each day, even the smallest step forward is victory, a reminder that you're stronger than the hurt. You will find joy and peace again. This journey is building a resilience in you, shaping you into someone who will not only will survive, but thrive. Hold on to hope. Victory is coming, and one day you too will began see beauty in the place of ashes.

My heart sends your heart a hug today.

REFLECTION |

As I am in pain today, God I need your help to just make a few steps. Help me to grieve, understand what has happen, and to feel joy and peace again.

STEP 1:

_____

_____

_____

_____

STEP 2:

_____

_____

_____

_____

STEP 3:

_____

_____

_____

_____

AFFIRMATION |

You may have taken _____, but you will not take what this family stands for. We may not understand why in this moment; however, we will be stronger because God will continue to give us strength, a heart of forgiveness, joy, and peace.

Put a family portrait below that reminds you of who your family was before the hurt. Keep declaring that you will be stronger, you can forgive, and you will continue to have joy and peace.

Place a photo of your
loved one(s) here

CHAPTER
Three

DEATH | THE NON-NEGOTIABLE

SHATTERED BUT NOT DESTROYED

Dear Journal

"

Today I am somewhere between the future and the past. Like standing at the top of the hill or being at the top of a roller coaster, what I know for sure is that I can't go backwards, although not being able to predict the future makes it all the more comforting.

"

Francesca

3 Chapter

DEATH | THE NON-NEGOTIABLE

Ecclesiastes 3:1-2 [KJV] To everything there is season, and a time to every purpose under the heaven; a time to be born, and a time to die, a time to plant, and a time to pluck up that which is planted.

After hearing the devastating news, I gathered myself enough to inform my sister, Diane, of what happened. Our family is large, so with one call, the news spread rapidly. Within 30 minutes my yard was full of family members offering support, though nothing could soothe the pain I felt.

The detective wanted to know who might have wanted to harm Francesca, and if she had any enemies. I answered the questions as best I could, though I was still in shock. I remember telling him that Francesca was pregnant. I learned later that her unborn child - a boy- had died with her. The detectives also questioned my family and strangely enough, everyone mentioned the same name when asked who they thought might be responsible for Francesca's death. He later asked me to meet him at Francesca's apartment so he could begin his investigation. He didn't want anything to be moved or tampered with.

I called the leasing office, gave the young lady my name and informed her that I was Francesca's mother. I asked for a key or some way to gain entrance into her apartment. When I arrived, I waited for the young lady to meet me and let me in. When I met her, she hugged me tightly and cried profusely. My heart broke for her. She told me that she had given Francesca information on how to get out of the relationship she was in. She shared with me that she had also been in an abusive relationship and tried to help my daughter as best as she could. She kept repeating, "I tried to help her." I could see she was still trying to process Francesca's death, just as I was.

As I stood in Francesca's apartment, surrounded by all her belongings, the reality of the situation hit me even harder - *she was really gone*. Her apartment was extremely small. It looked like a one-bedroom dollhouse. When

I walked in, the bathroom was on the right. She had left her jeans in the bathroom as if she had dressed a hurry. To my left was the living room. There was a small sofa, chair, lamp, and a table. On the table, there was information about domestic abuse. There was also an ultrasound picture of her baby, and pamphlets on health care for her and the baby.

As we grow up, we make our own blueprint of our lives. We think about our life expectations and setting timelines for different milestones. As young girls, we may imagine what we want our husband to look like, his height, the number of children we would have, what size house we would live in and what we would do in our careers. The one thing we never think about is - *death*, or the possibility of a phone call that could drastically change our lives forever. We never have conversations about death.

As parents, we take for granted that our children will outlive us. We live our lives focusing on the beginning date and the middle date, but the end date is left blank. We avoid having a conversation about death and live as though we have all the time in the world. We think our plans for tomorrow will wait for us to be ready. But death doesn't consider our hopes, dreams, or love. Death does not negotiate. It does not ask permission or wait until we are ready for it. It comes when it wills, disrupting our lives, and forcing us to face the reality of our own morality. Death comes without warning. It's final and absolute. It serves as a daily reminder that we are not in control.

Death is a bully. It was cruel to me, it forced its way into my life, my family's life, without warning or mercy. One day I was a mother with a daughter full of life and promise, and the next day I was faced with the harsh reality that she was gone forever. It didn't matter that I have a personal relationship with the Lord, that I preached the gospel, that I had faithfully served Him and others. There was no bargaining, no matter how long I cried, how desperate I felt, or how fervently I prayed.

Death left no room for compromise. In the aftermath, I found myself wrestling with God, questioning His fairness, and searching for answers that seemed just out of reach. "Lord, are you there? How could this happen to my daughter?" I asked again and again. I have been faithful, so why was this happening? It felt like a betrayal. Losing her was devastating enough, but the way she died made it so much worse. I had spent my life preaching a message of hope, yet I found myself trapped in a place of deep despair.

I forced myself to remember God's word, His promises and most of all His unconditional love. Psalm 34:19 [KJV] states, "Many are the afflictions of the righteous, but the Lord delivereth him out of them all." In my darkest moments, I held onto this truth, even when it felt like the deliverance was distant and the pain was all-consuming. Death had dealt a brutal blow, but it would not have the final say. Even in my brokenness, grace appeared as strength for the moment, and this allowed me to cling to the faith that God's love and his promises would sustain me through the storm.

When death came sneakily for my daughter there was nothing I could do to stop it. If she had been sick there would have been a warning. Death was non-negotiable for my daughter. It came abruptly for her, despite the life that she was carrying in her womb, the love she had and the future that she had hoped to live. Death came without warning and without mercy. It didn't offer a pause, reconsideration, or a way out. There was nothing she or anyone could do to change that. I learned this in the most brutal way possible.

I've replayed that moment in my mind countless times, trying to make sense of the senselessness, trying to understand how something so violent, so brutal, could steal away someone so full of life. I wrestled with the finality of it all. The pain of that realization is something I wouldn't want to wish on anyone. It's a pain that sits deep in my chest, a reminder of the empty void left behind.

Death is non-negotiable, but the love I hold for Francesca and the impact of her life on me and those that knew her, is something that death can never take away. It's what keeps me going.

Psalm 46:1 [KJV] states, "God is our refugee and strength, a very present help in trouble." This scripture is personal, it was written for me. It was God speaking directly to me, offering me comfort and assuring a safe place, a shelter, protection in the midst of the storm. He is my peace in the midst of my fears and in the midst of chaos. God is not only my refuge, but he is also my strength. There were days I was completely drained and felt as though I could not go on, but His power enabled me to endure, to persevere, and to get up. He is my very present help, my right now help. He is not distant, he is omnipresent - everywhere, he is not unaware, or unavailable.

God was and is, actively involved and immediately accessible in my trouble. God does not slumber or sleep. He knows the number of hairs on my head. God has shown himself to me. Through it all, I can depend on him, he is dependable and is always there, even in my darkest days, my most chaotic days God is dependable and is always there to offer solace.

As I write this story, my grief remains as fresh as ever, especially since no one has been brought to justice. My heart is shattered and while the pain is still excruciating, it has become more bearable over time. I know that if it wasn't for my belief in God, I would have fainted unless I believed in the goodness of the Lord in the land of the living. I would have lost myself completely.

Fainting doesn't always mean losing consciousness, sometimes, it means fainting in heart, in my belief, fainting in the word, and in the ministry that God has called me to fulfill. Without my faith, I could have drowned in depression. I could have tried to numb my pain using drugs or alcohol.

You may feel as though you are trapped in darkness, unable to see the light. But God is your protector, your navigator, and your GPS. He is your safe space, your place of refuge. He offers a space where you can cry, scream, or even break something without fear or judgment. Stay as long as you need to in this place, but remember, it is not permanent.

> **66** To everything there is a season,
> and a time to every *purpose*
> under the heaven: A time to be
> *born,* and a time to *die.* **99**
> ECCLESIASTES 3:1 KJV

REFLECTION |

Death is a non-negotiating force, a finality that cannot be bargained with and none of us can fully understand or control. Even in the midst of darkness and the pain of loss, faith can shine a light of hope. By trusting in God's plan, even when we don't fully understand it, we acknowledge that He alone is in control and has a greater purpose for each of us. Although the loss of our loved ones creates a deep ache and void in our hearts, placing our trust in God's divine plan and purpose can offer us the comfort and strength we need to endure our grief with hope.

CHAPTER
Four

THE FINAL GOODBYE

SHATTERED BUT NOT DESTROYED

Dear Journal

> "
>
> ## Thank God I found the good in goodbye.
>
> "

Francesca

4 *Chapter*
THE FINAL GOODBYE

Goodbyes are only for those who love with their eyes. Because for those who love with heart and soul there is no such thing as separation. - Rumi.

The last goodbye is something no mother should have to say to her child. It's a moment I never imagined I would face, and yet there I was, planning my daughter's funeral. Organizing a funeral is one of the most difficult tasks a parent could face; but, preparing for this during a global pandemic made these challenges even more daunting. The restrictions and uncertainty of COVID-19 added a layer of complexity that made an already heartbreaking situation feel nearly impossible. Restrictions on gatherings, social distant mandates, and fears about the virus loomed over every decision. The thought of not being able to honor her in the way she deserved weighed heavily on me. It felt like I had been robbed and cheated.

Her unborn son didn't have an identity, a name. It was almost as though he was viewed as an object. I felt a sense of loss for the life that could've been, for the future that was stolen before it even had a chance to begin. This was a double hit, a devastating blow that felt like I was losing the promise of a new generation. It was a sorrow that words couldn't fully express. I wanted to trust in the Lord, to hold on to my faith, but this was a true test, one that shook me to my core.

Nineteen days before Francesca's death, my daughter Lashara gave birth to my grandson AJ. They would've been seven months apart in age. Sometimes when I look at AJ, I wonder if the two of them would have been close cousins. While writing this, I feel a sense of guilt, even though Francesca was in her second trimester, he was a life that didn't have a voice and very little was ever spoken about him. I felt the child had been ignored with no voice because everything up until this point was about Franny.

The final goodbye wasn't just to my daughter, it was to the grandchild I would never know. The weight of this loss felt infinite and to further complicate my grief, the shooter remains at large. But I held onto the love that could never be taken away, the love that exists beyond goodbyes, beyond separation, and even beyond death. My mouth says, "I trust you, Lord," but my heart struggled to honor those words.

So many thoughts and emotions flooded my mind. So many unanswered questions. Who did this to my daughter? Why? What was the person thinking? I found myself consumed with anger toward the killer, imagining that the person who did this must be a cruel-hearted coward, selfish and heartless to shoot her, not just once, but twice in the heart. It was as though the killer wanted to ensure that she died without the compromise of survival. This new detail stirred my emotions even more. Her chest had to be rebuilt, her body patched up. I had to regroup because, at that moment, I was angry with the killer, and I didn't want my anger to turn to hatred.

I also found myself angry at Francesca for not acting on all the help that was offered to her, for not following through on her promise to take out a restraining order, not calling the abuse hotline, for procrastinating, not understanding the urgency, for going back into the relationship after leaving, for being blinded by love. I couldn't help but wonder why she was drawn back to his abuse. What was lacking in her life that this abuse somehow filled? Did I do something wrong as her mother? Why didn't she listen to the advice given by me and the apartment manager who also tried to help her? These questions haunted me, layering guilt on top of the grief and intensifying the pain of her loss. It felt as though I was digging into an already open wound, desperately trying to make sense of something that might never have a clear answer.

Franny had her own perspective of life and often felt like she could live her life the way she wanted, believing she was in control of her choices. However, she didn't always fully grasp the impact of her decisions or consider the potential outcomes. This mindset made her navigate life on her terms, but it also meant that she wasn't always prepared for the consequences that followed. She approached life with a sense of naïve independence, sometimes unaware of how her actions could affect not only herself, but also those who loved her.

The burden is even heavier when you're left to pick up the pieces. Making decisions and final arrangements in the wake of tragedy. Planning a funeral, and also dealing with legal matters, and managing the emotional fallouts. All these responsibilities fell on my shoulders, even though I played no part in the choices that led to this moment. I couldn't grieve clearly. My mind was full of the should haves, would haves, and could haves. In the midst of having to make unplanned decisions, her perspective made the process complex and painful. Why was I left to suffer the consequences of her poor decisions? I was furious that I had to be at the funeral home making these arrangements. Francesca's death affected everyone, our family, friends and those who loved and knew her. I often hear young adults say, 'I'm going to live my life the way I want to,' or 'this is my life, I'll do as I please.' *Please know that your life affects every person in your life.*

A few months before Francesca was murdered, she came to see me. She told me that she was being followed, also, that she knew and feared the stalker. She had witnessed him breaking into her car and stealing some items. She was too afraid to call the police and now, she feared for her life, because the stalker had verbally threatened her. Confronted with this troubling information, I inquired about the stalker, wanting to know specific details.

She told me how they met, how he had won her heart only to find out much later that he was already in a committed relationship. I immediately reprimanded her, reminding her of the way she was raised. My tone spoke of disappointment. She grew up in the church, in a Christian home, and the Bible was our guide book. Francesca quickly explained to me that she had broken the relationship off as soon as she found out his relationship status.

The compassion and the love of a mother set in, allowing me to comprehend the severity of the situation. My daughter had taken a bad turn and needed her mother's wisdom, love and guidance. My daughter was a very private person. For her to bring this information to me, she had to believe she was in harm's way. What I taught her was still there regardless of her choices. I told her to come back home, or I would help her find another place, and I warned her not to take this situation lightly. Unfortunately, she didn't move fast enough. That delay still haunts me.

Now, I felt drained and depleted, overwhelmed by everything that was happening. I just wanted to cover my ears, to shut out the world and the pain.

I needed help and support, and my wonderful friend RaiShaun Minor stepped in to support me. My daughter LaShara had just given birth, but she checked on me often. As I grappled with the overwhelming grief, another panic set in. I didn't have anything to bury my daughter in. The pandemic had closed so many stores and I was desperate to find something appropriate for Francesca.

RaiShaun and I drove around looking for a store, but nothing was open. Then, as if by divine intervention, my phone rang. It was my friend Sharon Oliver. She had just heard the devastating news and immediately called to express her condolences and offer her help. When I told her of my dilemma, not having anything to bury her in, Sharon didn't hesitate. She invited me to her boutique and blessed my daughter with a beautiful dress.

On the Tuesday evening that I had the heart-wrenching task of viewing my daughter, Franny, for the first time since her death, my husband and I were deeply disturbed by what we saw. We didn't think she looked like herself. Her skin was extremely dark, and we told the funeral director this wasn't how our daughter looked. My sisters observed the same thing; we didn't recognize her at all.

We worked with the personnel at the funeral home to fix her makeup, trying to bring back some resemblance of the Franny we knew and loved. After getting over that hurdle, all my emotions gushed out of control. It was like everything I had kept bottled up since the day I found out about her murder was unleashed and a relentless cycle of grief, a cycle with a broken knob that couldn't be turned off. I spent the better part of the evening crying uncontrollably, shaking my head in disbelief that she was really in that casket and that I was really there in that moment. It felt like something out of a movie, a surreal nightmare that I couldn't escape.

As I continued to gaze at her, through the haze of my tears, I noticed how beautiful she looked. All I could see was my girl. Her hair was styled perfectly, and she lay so still as if she didn't have a care in the world. Nothing moved or mattered to her, not even this day. Between the tears, I took in the details: the red dress she wore, adorned with a beautiful bow on the shoulder. It was absolutely stunning. It worked out well, despite my initial worries.

I wanted to bury her in a pink jumpsuit, but due to the reconstruction of her neck and chest, she had to wear a dress with a high neckline.

In the midst of it all, I don't know why, but I placed a white pearl ring on her finger. It was a small, almost instinctive gesture. Perhaps it was my way of giving her something in the face of ugliness, or maybe it was just one final act of love in a situation that had taken away so much, her future, even my dream of her walking down the aisle in marriage.

The evening was a mixture of disbelief, sorrow, and the cold, harsh reality that she was really gone. As much as I wanted to reject the truth there was no escaping it. The support from family and friends, though invaluable, couldn't soften the blow of seeing my daughter like this.

The viewing was open to the public on Wednesday, April 15, 2020, from 3 PM to 7 PM. However, due to restrictions, only 10 people were allowed in the room at a time, which included immediate family. Throughout the evening, I spoke to her friends, schoolmates, coworkers, and family that offered their words of comfort. Many said, "God knows best," while others reassured me, "God chose me because I was strong." Though their hearts were in the right place, their words didn't always bring the comfort they intended. Instead, they only stirred up my emotions. While I understood what they were trying to express, it still stung, because they still had their daughters. It felt like a hollow consolation in the face of such unbearable loss. Sometimes words aren't necessary. At that moment, I would've preferred a simple hug, just the quiet presence of someone acknowledging my pain.

There was one lady who stood out that night. She had a daughter younger than Francesca; I had ministered to her daughter many times at her request. Speaking about self-worth, saving herself for marriage, important things that a young woman needs to hear. That night, in front of my daughter's casket, this same mother confronted me. She had heard on the news that Francesca had been pregnant and was surprised. It was like she was questioning my integrity, because I had stayed on her daughter about purity. Her words were like a dagger – sharp and precise, hitting the target and intensifying an already unbearable situation. I didn't have the strength to fight back. My daughter had been murdered and yet, this was all she could say. The weight of her judgment in that moment was overwhelming, and all I could do was stand there, too broken to respond.

That was the hardest time, I cried so hard and long, I didn't realize I had so many tears. When the time came to say goodbye, only a few family members were still there, and I needed to cover my daughter, my baby girl and her unborn son; But I couldn't do it. I wasn't ready to release her, to let her go. I wasn't as strong as I wanted to be. I was still attached to her, unable to cut the cord. That was my baby girl. The staff at the funeral home was so patient, allowing me to take as much time as needed. I rubbed her hands, hugged her, and gave her a final kiss. I rubbed her stomach, symbolically hugging my grandchild. I hesitated, not wanting to release her. My hands shook as I finally covered her body knowing that once I did, it was final. I was crying uncontrollably, I was broken, shattered in a way I had never known before. Covering her was the most final act of goodbye and it left me empty and drained, feeling utterly lost. I felt as though my last connection with her was being severed. It hit me like a tidal wave, the undeniable reality that I would never see her again and that death is non-negotiable. Eventually, I covered her up, which made me think that every aspect of dealing with death is non-negotiable.

My husband had to leave early, not knowing that we would not be allowed to open the casket the next day, cover her and say our goodbyes. RaiShaun helped me to the car, and I cried to the top of my voice, she joined me. On the way home, we had to pull over and compose ourselves. I barely slept during the night, just dosing at times. I cried for the better part of the night, and woke up early to prepare for the funeral. I had exhausted all of my strength. I felt like a dead battery. I reminded the Lord that He said He would be my strength.

On Thursday, April 16, 2020, the day of Francesca's funeral, it felt like even the weather shared in my grief, reflecting the sorrow and heaviness that filled my heart. It was cold, extremely windy and damp. A gloomy day that seemed fitting for such a painful occasion. The biting cold mirrored the emptiness I felt inside. The wind, relentless and unpredictable, was like my mind, scattered and blown in every direction.

My son drove us to the funeral. It was the longest drive of my life. Each passing mile bought me closer to a reality I didn't want to face, and every second felt like eternity. It had to be a graveside service. At the grave, we shared a few words of expression. I had written something to say, but I couldn't bring myself to read it. My sister had to step in and read it for me. I watched my husband, his eyes fixed on the casket, tears streaming down his face as his arms hugged it.

As Pastor Rob preached the eulogy, I held on to my husband for dear life as if our combined strength could somehow bear the unbearable. At that moment, I saw no one else. The world around me had blurred, the only thing I could focus on was the devastating reality of what was happening. My eyes were hurting, burning, sore, they were swollen from crying so hard and long. The pain of my tears was as deep as the sorrow in my heart.

The funeral home had gone above and beyond for Francesca. They said she was too special for anything ordinary. When they told me it was time to get up, I wasn't ready to leave her behind, not like this. My body refused to let go. I had to be there, I stayed. I watched as they lowered her into the ground, her final resting place. I was paralyzed by the thought of leaving her there.

I didn't want to leave her behind, not like this. My body refused to move. My heart refused to let go. I had to be there watching, making sure they handled her with care until they covered her with the earth, until they sealed her away. Even then, I wasn't ready. That final goodbye was one I never wanted to say, a goodbye no mother should have had to give.

GONE BUT NEVER FORGOTTEN

Francesca Harris-Scarborough

15 NOVEMBER 1988 - 9 APRIL 2020

FOREVER IN ♥ MY HEART

Our Special Daughter,

It's sometimes hard to know why some things happen as they do.

For so much joy and happiness was centered around you.

It seems so hard to comprehend that you're no longer here, but all the happy memories will help to keep you near.

You're thought of often, Franny, with each mention of your name.

Death cannot change a single thing, the love will still remain.

Love,
Mom and Dad

Saying goodbye to a child is one of the mo
painful experiences a parent can endure. N
words or actions can fully erase the sorrow, y
there are ways to approach this goodbye wit
grace, compassion, and a sense of sacred hono
for the love you shared.

Remember...

It's Not Truly Goodbye.
Though it feels like a final parting, the love yo
share with your child is eternal. Love is a bon
that cannot be broken by time, distance, or eve
death. Your child lives on in your heart, in you
memories, and in every breath you take.

Embrace Every Memory.
Lean into the memories you hold. Each momen
every smile, and all the love you shared ar
treasures that remain with you forever. In thos
memories, you will find comfort, strength, an
even moments of joy as you honor your child'
life and legacy.

Lean Into Faith and the Promise of Reunion. Many find comfort in the hope of a heavenly reunion, knowing that, one day, you will be together again. Trust that God holds your child in His care and that His plans include eternal life and reunion beyond this earthly separation.

Trust That God Understands Your Pain. God knows the heartbreak of loss and the depth of a parent's love. In Isaiah 41:10, He promises, "Do not fear, for I am with you; do not be dismayed, for I am your God. I will strengthen you and help you; I will uphold you with my righteous right hand." Lean on this promise in your weakest moments, trusting that He will carry you through.

Take comfort in knowing that God walks with you, that your child's spirit endures, and that love is never lost. Though goodbye feels final, love makes it a gentle "See You Later" as you hold hope for the beautiful reunion to come.

CHAPTER
Five

A MOTHER'S LOVE

SHATTERED BUT NOT DESTROYED

Dear Journal

> **"**
> I can hear my mother's voice telling me things I wish I would've listened to.
> **"**

Francesca

5 Chapter
A MOTHER'S LOVE

A mother's love isn't bound by time or space. It weathers grief and loss holding firm, even when saying goodbye is the hardest thing. Even in death, a mother's love lingers still yearning to protect, comfort, and hold onto the child she nurtured or carried. This love is enduring, powerful, and undeniable.

Being a mother isn't defined solely by giving birth to a child. A mother is someone who would give her very life to save her child's. Mothers are chosen by God; handpicked to nurture, guide, and protect. My mother was chosen by God to be my mother, just as I was chosen to be the mother of my birth children and Francesca, whom I adopted. If you are a mother, know that God specifically selected you to be your child's mother. We are incubators, the sacred vessels, through which life enters this world.

The bond between a mother and child is profound because the mother is the protector beginning from the very moment that life starts in the womb. A mother's heart is to never willingly leave her child. If she does, it's due to circumstances beyond her control and not by choice; however, some do, unfortunately. Through good times and bad, a mother remains always wanting the best for her child.

If you've been adopted or separated from your biological mother, understand that the decision was made out of love because she wanted what was best for you, to give you the best chance in life. That's the essence of true love, that's the heart of a mother. My heart now aches for the mothers who had to give up their children for adoption or felt incapable of raising them due to mental, physical, or economic struggles. It's a pain that never fully leaves, a form of grief that lingers like losing a child. These mothers may carry a sense of guilt, regret or sorrow, knowing that they had to make an impossible choice for their child's well-being. It's a unique kind of heartache, where love and loss intertwine, and it can feel just as profound as the death of a child because it involves the absence of a connection that was never meant to be severed. I've come to realize that loss has many forms, and each one has a lasting impact on a mother's heart.

I understand that pain in a way I never thought I would. Though I didn't give birth to Francesca, I adopted her. Laying Franny to rest helped me grasp the deep agony a mother must feel when she surrenders or gives up her child. Today, I honor those mothers. I honor the memory of Francesca's birth mother, and I repent for prejudging or judging her or her life's journey. I now fully recognize the courage it must have taken to let her go. Releasing your child is directly parallel to losing a child. Both feel like death, and the results are long-term grief.

I honor every mother who loves fiercely, even when circumstances take her child away. A mother's love never dies; it endures through every sacrifice, every tear, and every hope she holds for her child's future.

Looking back at childhood memories only deepens the bond between a mother and her child. Even when they're gone, whether through death, leaving the nest, or just a short separation, it's hard for the mother. When I think back to my early memories with Francesca, or Franny as I lovingly called her, I am reminded of the day she came to live with me. She was a beautiful three-year-old girl with the sweetest chubby cheeks clinging to her older brother's hand, not wanting to let go. She leaned on him so much, as he took on the role of a protector, telling her that she would be alright, and assuring her that I would take good care of her. Even with his reassurances, she was struggling, so he gently but firmly told her that she had to stay. It was a tearful separation, but after he left, she began to explore her new surroundings. She appeared to be shy and didn't speak much, but when she did it was clear how articulate she was.

At the time, I was Aunt Shirley, her biological aunt. I introduced her to my children, Rob and Lashara, who made every effort to welcome her and show her that this new family would be *her* family. I showed Francesca to her room, showing her the new clothes and the toys, I bought for her. I wanted to do everything I could to make her feel at home. But when bedtime came, despite the pretty new nightgown I had picked out, she clung to her worn out footie pajamas. Those pajamas weren't just clothing to her, they were a connection to her past, her family, and the life she had known. I let her keep them and sleep in them for as long as she needed, because they provided a sense of security, and an anchor in an unfamiliar world.

The small seemingly ordinary moments become woven into the fabric of a mother's heart. Holding their hand on the first day of school, comforting them when they fall. Every smile, every cry, every whispered "I love you mommy," is etched into a mother's memory forever. With Francesca, I remember her as a little girl, full of curiosity and wonder, asking questions about the world, playing make believe, and always keeping me on my toes.

For many months, I was still Aunt Shirley to her, even though I had stepped into the role of her mother. At age four, Francesca developed pink eye one day out of nowhere, and everything changed. Both of her eyes became swollen and sore. She couldn't see, and I cared for her through the pain, holding her in my lap, comforting her as if she were a baby. In the midst of her discomfort and tears, she cried *"Mommy"* instead of "Aunt Shirley." The joy I felt in that moment was indescribable. It was like hearing a baby say their first word, but this word carried so much weight. It was a turning point. That day I didn't just act as her mother, I became her mother in her heart.

This was such a blessing to me because it meant she felt safe, secure, and loved. Our bond was growing, but more importantly, she chose this relationship on her own terms. Finally, she was ready to fully be identified as my child. Francesca came and told me that she wanted my name. All her father and I needed to do was sign our names on the dotted line. She chose to keep her last name Harris and add Scarborough, creating the name Harris-Scarborough. It was her way of honoring and acknowledging her birth family, while embracing her new identity with us.

I was incredibly proud of her maturity and understanding. All of my efforts didn't go unnoticed. She understood the depth of the love I had for her, the love of a mother. A mother sacrifices, nurtures, disciplines when needed, forgives time and time, and sees beyond mistakes to the heart of her child. In the same way, God's love is mirrored for us, unconditional, unwavering, and eternal. Francesca felt that love, because she chose to be identified with it in her own way. A mother's love is so important. When absent, there's like a hole in the heart that needs to be filled and healed. Every child needs their mother.

From time to time, mostly in her early teens, Franny would talk about her birth mother. She would tell me, "*I can hear her voice, but I can't remember her face. I wish I could remember what she looked like*". She never stopped missing her birth mother.

As I write this, I realize God placed Franny in my care because our life shared many similarities. Our hurts and disappointments mirrored one another. We had so much in common. I vividly remember being in the third grade when, out of nowhere, my father told me I would be leaving that afternoon to stay temporarily with an elderly neighbor. I had never met her before, but my father explained she was afraid to stay alone at night, while her husband was hospitalized, and since they had no children of their own, she needed help. Our family lived on a farm, and my parents had seventeen children. That day, my mother was washing clothes in a tin tub, scrubbing with a washboard, and I was trying my best to be strong, but I was scared. They could tell, so they decided to send My sister Joan with me for comfort. Joan was three years older than me, and we were meant to stay with the neighbor only until her husband was discharged from the hospital. Unfortunately, her husband passed away, and what was supposed to be temporary, turned into something more permanent for me. Joan was eventually sent back home, but I remained with the neighbor.

Just like Franny, I packed my things to go live with someone I had never met. I didn't want to leave my family, but I had no choice. I longed for my mother. A mother has a special touch, scent, and even before a child can open their eyes, they know who their mother is. Over time, I bonded with my neighbor. She began to take care of me, doing the motherly things my own mother couldn't do for me. I grew to love her just as she grew to love me. We both had a need that we fulfilled in one another.

I would visit home daily when the weather was good, staying for a few hours in the evening. My mother was an incredible woman, a mother who sacrificed for her seventeen children, putting her life on hold for them, but somewhere a disconnect happened between us. I remember wanting my mother to want me. I believe she loved me, but my teenage years were hard because I didn't have her hand of guidance or motherly influence. Though my mother was a wonderful God-fearing woman, there were moments when the silent grief of my heart caused a disconnection during our visits, and our communication was strained and rather awkward.

Now, thinking back, Francesca struggled deeply during her teenage years. There was a longing, a sadness I could see in her eyes. As I reflect on our journey, I understand more of what she must have felt, the feelings of sadness, isolation, and the pain of disconnection. I also recognized the feelings of void in her heart and the desire to be loved and validated by her birth mother. *If you are a parent, it's important to listen to your child's heart, look into your child's eyes and watch your child's behaviors.*

Many days, Franny often wanted to be alone, retreating to her own world. It felt as though an unbreakable wall was between us. Then, there were moments when she would let me in. Those days, she was vibrant, outgoing and full of energy. Her laugh was contagious. Like most teenagers she was moody. Franny had expensive taste and loved to shop. She was always drawn to elegant and luxurious things. She was also ambitious. When she set her mind to do something, she pursued it with unwavering determination; sometimes she received rewards and other times this got her into trouble.

When Franny was sixteen, I made the difficult decision to take her to visit her birth mother. I wanted her to have the chance to see her mother's face, ask questions that lingered in her heart, and hopefully find the closure she needed. I thought it might bring some peace, but in the end, I think it did more harm than good. At the time, her birth mother was struggling with drug addiction and was staying at a rehab center. We waited in a small, dimly lit room for her to come out. Franny was visibly nervous. She stayed close to me. I tried to reassure her, telling her everything would be okay, but even I was anxious about what was about to unfold.

When her birth mother finally entered the room, she was casual, almost arrogant, and clearly uncomfortable. She spoke briefly, nervously asking Franny how she had been. The energy in the room was tense, but then the conversation took a turn that I hadn't expected.

Franny began to ask questions that she had been waiting to ask. With a soft voice filled with hope and fear she asked her mother "*Do you miss me?*" Her birth mother without hesitation answered, "no". The pain in that single word was palpable, cutting through the room like a knife. Franny, braver than

I realized, continued, *"Do you ever think about me?"* Once again, her birth mother replied with a simple, cold "no." In the midst of an emotionally charged conversation, I could feel my heart breaking for Francesca. Her emotions were raw and intense, bouncing from one feeling to another. It was as though she carried a deep burden, and I could sense the longing for reassurance in her voice, but it didn't end there. Just when I thought the conversation had reached its peak, Francesca, with trembling lips, asked one more question, perhaps the one that mattered the most to her: *"Do you ever think of me on my birthday?"* Her birth mother's response was devastating: "No, it's just another day."

I couldn't take it anymore. I gently grabbed Franny's hand and began leading her out of the room, away from the pain that was too much for her to bear. But before we left, I turned back. The anger and sadness inside me boiled over, and I couldn't stay silent. "Shame on you," I said, "how could you treat her like that? How could you hurt her like that?" I had a few more choice words for her. But the damage had been done.

When we got to the car, I hugged Franny tightly and told her how much I loved her, how I would always be there for her. She laid her head on the window and wept as though she was mourning a loss, as though this was the end. I sat there feeling helpless, wondering if I had made the wrong choice by taking her to visit her mom. That was the first time she had seen her birth mom since I had adopted her, and the last time before we attended her funeral.

Looking back, I realize now that Franny's birth mother did what she knew. She didn't have a relationship with her own mother and didn't have the capacity to offer Franny the love and connection she craved. Her answers, while hurtful, came from a place of emotional emptiness, not malice. She simply didn't have anything to give, and in the end, it was Franny who bore the brunt of that painful reality. Feeling disconnected is a horrible thing. It strips away purpose and leaves you in a place of limbo. When you are disconnected from those you love, it's as if you're not truly living. You're like a lamp unplugged, no longer fulfilling your intended purpose. You have the potential to shine but something is missing. That was how it felt with Franny at times. As a teenager I experienced the same disconnect.

This disconnect didn't just weigh heavily on her, it crushed me, too. As a mother, the feelings of abandonment, rejection, and separation are very real. When the connection between you and your child weakens, it feels like a part of your soul is torn away. I wanted so desperately for her to know that my love for her was unconditional, that it wasn't dependent on her behavior or choices, that it was unlimited. I loved her with all my heart, but no matter what I did, I couldn't always bridge the gap she felt. That was heartbreaking.

Perhaps you can identify with this story. Maybe you've felt the pain of disconnection or the deep need for love that you couldn't quite grasp. Maybe you struggle to understand why things happened the way they did or why love sometimes feels just out of reach. It's a pain that lingers in your heart. But through it all, there's one thing I want you to know - a mother's love should be unconditional. It is a love that has no strings attached, it's a love that says, "I have your back no matter what." This love is real.

A mother's love determines the emotional stability of a child. It builds trust, self-confidence, and self-esteem. If you've never experienced separation, adoption, or disconnection, it may be difficult to understand the depth of the effect it can have on a person, whether a baby, a teen, or even an adult. There's a reason why things happen to us, and many times we spend our lives wondering why or reacting to the pain it caused. I remember spending time watching how my siblings interacted with my mother, wishing I was in their place.

At the time my neighbor died, I was married and had my first child. I felt more disconnected than ever. I turned to the church mothers for guidance and nurturing, even though they were great women, they had their own families. I found myself searching for my mother in them. Have you ever read the story, '*Are you, my mother?*,' the one where the bird searches for his mother. Like Franny, I knew who my mother was, but I didn't know how to reach her in the way I needed. No one could replace that need, not my husband, not my children. It's a love that holds us even in the moments when we feel abandoned or rejected. Just like God's love, my love for Francesca remained steadfast through the highs and the lows, through the struggles and times of disconnect.

In the end, I believe that love, in its truest form, is about showing up even when it feels impossible. It's about being fully present in the midst of pain, knowing that while we may not be able to fix everything or heal every wound, we can still offer the kind of love that says, "I am here, and I will never leave you." That is the love I tried to give Francesca, even when the distance between us seemed impossible to resolve. When every instinct told me to pull away in the face of overwhelming grief, I chose to lean into love instead, step by step.

To those reading this, I want you to know that no matter how disconnected or broken you feel, there is a love that never wavers. You are seen, you are loved, and you are held by something greater than your pain. There is a mother's love, unwavering and constant and above all there is God's love which is unshakable, and always present. Let that be your anchor, even in the darkest moments.

REFLECTION |

I encourage you to put together a collage of happy moments and reflect on the blessing God gave you when you birthed or adopted, _____. Think of special moments you had together from all stages of their life. What did they love to eat, wear, and want to be or became? I am learning that Franny wanted to become a writer. As I went through her private items, I found she had had a love for writing. Franny had even signed up for a class and purchased an ISBN for her book. When I read her journal and she expressed her thoughts if anyone would read her book or think it was good. I reflected back to my own thoughts as I am writing this book. I would have never guessed that I would pick up her mantle and become an author.

No matter what happened, no one can take away the essence of who your child was. Through the grief, take time to remember the good of who they were and if you are like me, I am grateful that God allowed me to be a mom to Franny. The final circumstances of her life will NEVER take that away.

AFFIRMATION |

"Today, I choose to remember all the good things about my precious child. Their laughter that filled the room, their smile that could light up any day, and the way they embraced life with such pure joy. I cherish the moments we shared—the little victories, the deep conversations, the hugs that felt like home. Though my heart aches with their absence, I find comfort in the love they gave so freely and the beautiful memories we created together. I honor their spirit by celebrating the impact they made, and I hold onto the love that will forever connect us. I am grateful for every moment I was blessed to share with them."

"He will wipe every tear from t.
eyes. There will be no more de
or mourning or crying or pa

Memories

let did

for the old order of
things will pass away."
REVELATION 21:4 NIV

CHAPTER Six

GRIEF | THE UNINVITED GUEST

SHATTERED BUT NOT DESTROYED

Dear Journal

> **"**
>
> Grief is uncontrollable and healing may seem impossible.
>
> **"**

Shirley

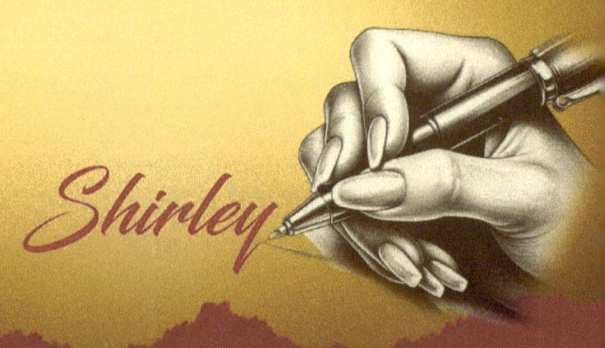

6 Chapter
GRIEF | THE UNINVITED GUEST

G rief is an inevitable, deeply personal, and traumatic experience. It is something we all must confront at some point in life. Whether it's the loss of a loved one, a friend or even an unexpected life change. Grief arrives unannounced, and its impact is profound.

The grief of losing Franny to murder is unexplainable and it was unpredictable. I didn't know what to expect after the funeral. I struggled coming to terms that she was really gone, that her final resting place, the cemetery, was now her new address. It became a place I visited regularly. For many months I would drive there, sometimes just sitting in my car, lost in thought. I knew she was no longer there in spirit, but my heart struggled to accept it. Even though I understood that her soul had moved on, my heart refused to let go. Her new address represented the void, a finality, when the curtain is drawn after the last act, *except,* I had no standing ovation to give. Putting flowers on her grave on her birthday was my way of remembering her. Cleaning off her grave is my way of taking care of her and the way I worked through my grief.

Grief arrived as an uninvited guest. The uninvited guest who murdered my daughter, entered our lives without warning or permission. He didn't knock; he barged in, unwelcomed and unapologetic, without warning or permission to take residence in every corner of my heart. The same way he worked his way into Francesca's life, the uninvited guest came into our family's life as an intruder, with force and determination.

In 2018, my ninety-one-year-old mother as she was beginning to transition asked me to release her and let her go. She told me that she was ready and tired. She needed to rest. As painful as it was, I agreed and released her into the hands of the Lord, asking Him to take her with Him, and to ease her pain. Even though it hurt, I felt more prepared. My mother had raised seventeen birth children, she was blessed to have many grandchildren and great grandchildren and great-great-grandchildren. My mother lived an active life, a full life. With my mother's death, there was a sense of closure. I had the gift of being by her side, holding her hand and saying goodbye. It was heartbreaking, but it also felt like a peaceful transition, a final chapter that we shared together.

With Francesca, I felt robbed and cheated. I had no say so concerning her departure. No parent expects to outlive their child. No mother should have to bury her child. I felt as though her death was out of sequence. Life has dealt me a blow no mother should ever have to endure. Burying my daughter was not something I was supposed to do. It feels like someone flipped the script of life, reversing the roles in the most painful, unimaginable way.

Unlike the transition of my mother. I wasn't prepared for the uninvited guest's arrival, but yet he was there, demanding my attention, changing everything. The uninvited stranger entered my life, catching me off guard, unlike anything I've ever experienced. I didn't know how long he would stay or how deeply his presence would affect me. He made himself at home, disrupting my routines, disrespecting boundaries and my plans, clouding joyful moments, and lingering longer than anyone could anticipate. Grief didn't care about timing, convenience, or my ability to cope. He didn't care that mentally and emotionally, I felt as though I was at my wits end. He simply arrived and settled in occupying every room in my house.

Grief doesn't come with a manual or instructions on how to deal with it. One moment I thought I had a handle on it, and the next moment it was as though someone had pulled the rug right out from under me with no warning. Much like a guest who overstays its welcome, grief lingers, its presence is felt in the quiet moments of the day, in the memories that unexpectedly resurface, and in the spaces, the empty chair once filled by Francesca.

My initial meeting with grief was overwhelming. I remember coming home one evening crying for no reason for about four hours. My husband consoled me as best he could but the pain overpowered all his words, his hugs, his comforting. Hearing her name or hearing someone talk about her at times was painful. I remember going to my granddaughter's track and the coach shot the gun for the runners to run. Hearing the gunshot took me to a place of sorrow that I didn't know existed. I completely lost it, I had a melt down and was comforted by strangers. It's like standing face-to-face with an unfamiliar figure, someone whose presence you didn't anticipate yet cannot ignore. Much like meeting a stranger, you feel awkward, unsure, and vulnerable. It made me wonder how long this relationship will last and whether I will ever be the same again.

Grief doesn't have a singular form or pattern, much like no two strangers are alike. Sometimes it's loud and consuming, overwhelming your imagination and senses, making it difficult to breathe. Other times, it's quiet, lurking into the background, waiting for moments of stillness to remind me of its presence. It comes and goes on his own terms, and there is no way to prepare for the way it would change. It became a new rhythm in my life, one that I had to move with and dance to its beat.

Grief is often confusing, it's like riding a roller coaster. One minute you're on the top, seconds later, you're at the bottom. I resisted it, fought against its presence, but the moment I heard the words, "I'm sorry, your daughter was found dead," I found that it wasn't going anywhere. It was there to stay; and in an unsettling way, it starts to feel like a companion.

The transformation from stranger to companion is gradual, almost imperceptible. Grief which once felt unbearable, begins to take on a different shape. Instead of fighting it, I was learning how to coexist with it. I started to recognize the pattern of its presence before it appeared. The tears, the sorrow, the anger didn't stop. Neither did the flutter in the heart, nor the lump in the throat. They became familiar. It reminded me of an old friend who showed up uninvited but was expected, nonetheless. There is a strange companion that comes when certain things happen in life, you don't call for them, but somehow, they know when to come. I have been learning patience, resilience, and compassion for everyone. Before Francesca's death, I was quick to judge. The man standing at the stoplight asking for a dollar for a drink, the addict, the homeless, I judged them without knowing their burdens. Now, I realize the common denominator in all of our stories is pain and loss. Grief teaches you that.

Grief may not always be death. For some, it may be a divorce, or the loss of a child, a job, a pet, or something that once held deep personal value.

It's that unexpected event that changes the course of life. So, I ask you, who or what is the intruder in your life that has caused you grief, pain or disappointment? What unexpected presence has stopped you from dreaming, hoping, or believing in something more? How has this uninvited guest reshaped your journey?

Even as grief attempts to steal my joy and drain my spirit, there is a power greater than grief. The power of God, the power of hope. He is the greater one that lives on the inside of me, the one that won't let me drown in pity or depression. He is the Author and finisher of my faith, my refuge, my very present help in the time of trouble. In the midnight hour, God is the only one that doesn't slumber nor sleep, he hears my cry, and he loves me and is concerned about me.

This companionship with grief is not one I would ever choose, but it became a reality I must accept. I now learn to carry it with me in a way that allows me to function, to live my life even in its presence. There are times I felt the experience of being both empty and full at the same time. It's a strange sensation, almost like a chemical imbalance. It's like having dual emotions. On one hand, the emptiness comes from the absence of Francesca, her laughter, her presence, and her spirit. That void is an ache that's lodged in the center of my heart and no matter how much time passes by it never fully goes away. I might smile on the outside, but it often masks the pain inside. For those who haven't experienced deep loss, it's difficult to understand the true effects of grief. It doesn't just hurt emotionally. It drained me, left me often feeling alone as though something vital had been taken from me. There's an empty space inside of me that seems to grow, making the loss feel even larger and more consuming. It keeps me in search of finding purpose and hope, yet those things feel so distant. Grief is like a lingering fog that never fully clears. It hovers over everything, making it harder to see the path ahead.

Yet on the other hand, there is a fullness that exists alongside this emptiness. The fullness is tied to the memories, the love and the bond I have with Francesca that will never fade. It's the sense that even though Francesca is not physically present with me, she is still with me in spirit, in her weird but unique laughter, in the softness of her voice, through her dreams and visions she spoke about in her diary, her beauty inside out, those cherished memories that fill my heart and brings comfort to me. It becomes both a burden and a bridge, a burden because it reminds me of the loss, but yet a bridge because it helps me stay connected to her. I believe this is God's love and comfort, His way of showing me that even in the bad there is something good. It's God's way of balancing the immense pain of loss with the equally immense capacity to love and remember.

The grief I experienced often felt like an unbearable weight, but the fullness of God's love provided solace, offering moments of peace and connection amidst the sorrow. Grief is teaching me that it is okay to be empty and full at the same time. I can mourn the loss while celebrating the love that lives on. Francesca's absence may have left an empty chair, but her memory fills the space around it, keeping her spirit alive in my heart.

As with any new relationship, I began to learn the ways to grieve over time. I started to understand how it manifests, and how it flows. There are moments when grief feels almost like an old friend, familiar, though still painful. But just when I think I figured it out, it shifts again, revealing new depths of emotion and sorrow I didn't know was there. Grief, like a stranger, kept me on the edge, constantly reintroducing itself to me in ways I could not predict.

One day it's a stranger, then it became my companion. It walks with you through every part of your life, shaping who you are or becoming. It becomes a part of your story affecting not just your heart but my body, weighing me down physically, attacking my health. One day I went to visit my friend at work, when I walked into her office, she started praying for me, praying for the grief she saw behind my eyes. Grief had become abusive and was controlling my life. It held me hostage, not allowing me to attend functions and celebrations. Grief kept me isolated as if it wanted me for itself, to the point where I would try to bargain with myself. Grief had me boxed in. There was no escape.

The shock of Francesca's murder hit me in ways I never could have prepared for. Death by violence is sudden, brutal and impossible to rationalize. The grief I experienced was compounded with questions that had no answer, and by a profound sense of injustice. It has no closure. Grief also asked questions I never thought I would have to answer. It forced me to confront feelings of loss, longing, and despair. Grief challenges the very core of who you are. It asks you to adjust to a new normal life, a life where the person is no longer present.

Coming to terms felt like an impossible task, like walking in a dark room where there is no light. At times, I found myself questioning God, asking why He allowed this to happen to my daughter, who had so much life yet to live. How could I come to terms with something so painful?

Grief is often described as a journey. To me it feels more like a battle - an unrelenting struggle to survive. It reminds me of a surfer, riding the waves of pain, sorrow, and longing that wash over you day after day. It is something you don't ever get over or move on from, but something I'm learning to live with. It has been and will continually be my teacher. I just simply follow its instructions. Sometimes I'm instructed to cry, so I cry, sometimes I just moan, Sometimes I retreat to a quiet safe space.

I feel as though grief has become my partner, not one I would choose but one that is needed to navigate my new journey.

Coming to terms with the death of my daughter, Francesca, and the weight of grief is an unimaginable journey, one that feels endless and insurmountable; a process unlike any other grief I had experienced before. The loss of my daughter or of a child is a profound rupture of the natural order of life, a break in the path you would travel together. It is a pain that not only sears the soul but also alters the fabric of existence, leaving a void that feels impossible to fill. It was not simply the loss of her physical presence, but the loss of the future I had imagined for her and the many shared moments and her unfulfilled dreams that will never come to pass.

As a mother you imagine so many milestones for your children, the first steps, the school graduations, the first loves. Grief has stolen the joy from these moments. For me, that dream will never be realized, and that truth is a constant ache in my heart. I found weddings particularly difficult to attend.

Seeing her rolled down the aisle instead of her father escorting her down the aisle was a painful reminder that the future was done. I often find myself envisioning how it might have been. I picture Francesca in a beautiful gown, glowing with joy and excitement, her smile lighting up the room. I imagine helping her pick out the dress, fussing over details with her, sharing that special bond between mother and daughter, as we prepare for one of the biggest days of her life. But instead of those memories, I am left with emptiness, knowing that these moments would never come. It feels like a part of me was lost, a part of my future that is now forever out of reach.

It's not just the wedding that haunts me. There are so many other dreams and milestones that will never be fulfilled, like a chapter left unwritten in the story of her life. Seeing her find her career path, watching her grow as a woman, and some day, perhaps becoming a mother herself, watching her hold her first child were dreams I cherished. Instead, she carried her murdered child within her, a haunting reality that intensifies my grief. Knowing I will never witness her walk through those doors of life, never see her reach those beautiful moments is a wound that never truly heals. As a mother, the absence of these moments feels unbearable, like holding onto a puzzle that will never come together because the most precious pieces are lost forever.

Today, each page of pain will now be met with peace, reminding me that love transcends the suffering, and that Francesca's memory will not end in hopelessness, but joy and serenity. Ecclesiastes 9:5-6 [KJV] states, *"For the living know that they shall die: but the dead know not anything, neither have they any more a reward; for the memory of them is forgotten. Also, their love, and their hatred, and their envy, is now perished; neither have they any more a portion forever in anything that is done under the sun."* This is my reassurance that Francesca is resting, she doesn't know what happened to her and my grandchild. This really consoled me. She is not worried about me, or about what happened to her.

Although grief is the uninvited guest, the sorrow that consumes me becomes a constant reminder of the life she lived and could have lived. Partnering with grief is not a choice. It's like shaking hands with a stranger, knowing they are not here to stay, unsure of what this new relationship will bring. I didn't want it, but there it stands, a presence I couldn't ignore, yet knowing that I will have to learn to live with it. We may ask what if, and why. But in the end, there is no deal to be made.

John 11:35 KJV

Jesus wept.

1 Thessalonians KJV 4:13-14

But I would not have you to be ignorant brethren, concerning them which are asleep, that ye sorrow not, even as others which have no hope. For if we believe that Jesus died and rose again, even so them also which sleep in Jesus will God bring with him.

Losing a child can feel like the ultimate test of faith, patience, and strength. Grief is uncontrollable, and healing may seem impossible. Yet, there are some small steps and comforting moments that can help bring glimpses of peace, connection and renewed strength. Though the journey is painful, hold on to the heart mender tips throughout this book that guided me and are still guiding me towards healing, one step at a time.

GIVE YOURSELF PERMISSION TO GRIEVE FULLY

Heart Mender

Remember there is NO "right way to grieve" and there is NO time limit. Allow yourself to feel whatever comes-anger, sadness, even numbness. Remember your feelings are valid.

SEEK SPIRITUAL STRENGTH AND MEANING

Heart Mender

Find strength by leaning deeply into your faith. Look to Jesus, who is the Author and Finisher of our faith. Turn to prayer and immerse yourself in God's word. Draw close to him allowing His presence to uplift and carry you through even the hardest moments. Let His promises be your anchor and his love your constant guide.

LEAN ON SUPPORTED PEOPLE

Heart Mender

Surround yourself with family, friends, or support groups who understand the gravity of your loss. A grief counselor or support group of parents who have lost children, can offer this sense of community and understanding.

CREATE A MEMORIAL OR TRIBUTE

Heart Mender

Honoring your child's memory in a tangible way can be healing. Create a memory box, plant a tree. These acts honor their legacy and create a sense of connection.

FIND COMFORT IN ROUTINE, BUT ALLOW FLEXIBILITY

Heart Mender
While maintaining daily routines can offer some stability, take your time. Take a break when you need to. Take things one day at a time and embrace the small steps. Celebrate moments of peace and allow space for setbacks.

JOURNAL YOUR FEELINGS AND MEMORIES

Heart Mender
Writing can help you process complex emotions and keep your child's memory alive. Write about happy moments, the difficult feelings and anything else that's on your heart. Journaling can be a safe place to express things you may not be able to share aloud.

PRACTICE SELF COMPASSION AND FORGIVENESS

Heart Mender
Loss often brings feelings of guilt, questioning, and self-blame. Remind yourself that grief is a process, not something you "get over." Offer yourself the same compassion you would extend to others and forgive yourself for things left unattended. Forgive others.

❝ The is no *pain* like the broken heart of a *grieving* mother. ❞
UNKNOWN

CHAPTER
Seven

KISSING FROGS | THE ILLUSIONS AND LIES

SHATTERED BUT NOT DESTROYED

Dear Journal

"

What is love? I honestly don't think anyone has felt it to its greatest extent and I feel like I want to. The most important thing I've learned is that to everything there is a bigger picture. Things are never as they though may seem on the surface.

"

Francesca

7 Chapter
KISSING FROGS | THE ILLUSIONS AND LIES

Have you ever found yourself waiting for love to come along and make everything right? Maybe, like many of us, you grew up with stories of Prince Charming, believing someone would sweep you off your feet, and you would live happily ever after. But as life goes on, we often find that real love is far more complicated than the fairy tales we once believed in.

Take the story of sleeping beauty, lying in a deep sleep, waiting for her prince to awaken her with a kiss. Her entire fate depended on someone else to save her, just as we sometimes wait for someone to come into our lives, rescue us, heal our wounds, and complete our happily ever after.

Francesca, like Sleeping Beauty, was waiting for her Prince Charming, but her longing was about more than just romance. It went deeper, stemming from the rejection and abandonment she experienced as a child, left by her birth parents. That void followed her through life, and she spent her years trying to fill that space. The fairytale she held onto wasn't just about love but about being rescued. It wasn't only a prince she was waiting for, it was her birth parents, whom she hoped would one day return and reunite her family. She waited for them to come back and make things right, and when they didn't, she sought the same from romance. This deep seeded desire shaped Francesca's view of love and relationship, influencing her expectations.

As Tina Turner once asked, "What's love got to do with it?" Love can be beautiful, but it can also be blinding, especially when it's entangled with lies and illusions. Sometimes we are so captivated by the idea of love that we overlook red flags, convincing ourselves that the person in front of us is our fairy partner, when in reality they are far from it. Like Tina saying love can feel like a "second-hand emotion" when its built-on illusions instead of truth.

Lies make it easier to cling to fantasies rather than facing reality. Well, when that illusion shatters, we are left wondering if any of it was real, struggling to accept that true love is grounded in honesty and respect- not just sweet words and empty promises. So, what does love have to do with it? Everything and nothing. Real love, the kind worth holding onto, doesn't need to be disguised or false. It stands strong and genuine in truth.

Ladies, life doesn't end. After the illusion ends and your eyes are open:

1. **Began to Embrace Reality**
God gives grace, so give yourself grace. Accepting that he wasn't who you thought he was, is painful but is also freeing you, now you can begin to heal.

2. **Reclaim Your Worth**
Don't let his actions diminish your value. His behavior is a reflection of him not you. Stand firm in your self-worth and know you deserve honesty and respect.

3. **Release the Illusion**
Let go of the idea of "what could have been" clinging to the illusion of a "prince" keeps you tied to something that wasn't real. Focus on what is real and healthy for you.

4. **Lean into Self-love**
Show yourself the love you deserve. Rediscover your passions, invest in your friendships and nurture your dreams. The love you seek starts within you.

5. Guard Your Heart Wisely

Take this as experience as a lesson not a loss. Move forward, trust your instincts, set healthy boundaries, and take your time getting to know someone's true character.

6. Trust in a Brighter Future

Believe that this setback is paving the way for something better. You have the power to move beyond this, stronger and wiser.

What *illusions* and *lies* are you being told?

If only you would then
I wouldn't have to react badly

This (abuse) is a family matter; no
one needs to know about it

I will hurt myself if you leave me

I do this (abuse) because I love you

Your family or friends cant be trusted,
you can only trust me

I lied to protect you

You are such a...

What *illusions* and *lies* are you believing?

CHAPTER
Eight

LOVE IS BLIND | IGNORING RED FLAGS

SHATTERED BUT NOT DESTROYED

Dear Journal

"

I feel so burnt out. Sometimes it's like nothing you ever do is good enough. The other day his mother asked me what I saw in him and honestly after tonight I don't know.

"

Francesca

8 Chapter
LOVE IS BLIND | IGNORING RED FLAGS

We've all heard the phrase, "love is blind," and for many it holds a painful truth. When we fall in love our emotions can cloud our judgment, leading us to overlook red flags, convincing ourselves that things will get better, or that he will get better. We start to make excuses for his behavior. Love has a way of sweeping us off our feet, making the world seem beautiful, but in the midst of beauty, love can also blind us. When we fall in love with our eyes closed, we embrace only the fantasy, the idealized version of love where everything works out, no matter the challenges.

Francesca wrote that *"Things are never as though they may seem on the surface. You have to get to the bottom of everything. It's like I missed everything that was so clearly in front of my face, and I wish I could go back and live my life the way I should be living it. As luxurious as I love to be, I could be way more if I had just gotten the bigger picture..."*

Her words reveal a deep sense of regret as she reflects on her life. She longed to live life differently, by her own values, her beliefs, and by her upbringing. She acknowledged that she had strayed from those foundations, missing what was clearly in front of her all along. I ask you, "Is there a bigger picture that you're overlooking or have been overlooking?"

It's time to open our eyes to understand real love. Real love is the kind of love that nurtures and sustains, a love that is grounded in truth. It requires us to see the person for who they truly are, recognizing the imperfections, and confronting the reality of the relationship instead of holding onto a fairytale relationship we may have constructed in our minds that doesn't reflect the truth.

Can you identify with any of the signs Francesa wrote about in her journal? Have you missed any red flags, excused behavior, or ignored truths that were right in front of you?

Francesca's story is a reminder that love, while beautiful, must be based on honesty and reality, not fantasies we create in our minds. I pray her story inspires you to love with your eyes wide open. Like in the fairytales, he started out making her feel like she really was the princess. Franny wrote, *"The first year that I knew you, you were sweet and affectionate and kind and caring. You were always with me, we were inseparable. Then after a few months, I saw less and less of you. The second year your personality started to come out some for real. I saw the ugly side of you. It surprised me. When you hide yourself, the real you, you never give a person a chance to really love you. And that's all you ever wanted. Really that's all anybody ever wants. And I always wondered why you never wanted anyone to know your name. Your name may be_____ no one will ever know. The other day his mom asked me "what I saw in him," and honestly after tonight, I don't know. He refused to help me take out the trash. What is he good for?"*

I'll have a good memory of us and then it gets ruined by something bad that happened. Like I'll think about sex with you, the need to take it more seriously and make it mean something. Even though you were my only partner, you were partners with other people. I don't want that any more, I want it to be just me. I could get use to this man, combing and oiling my hair, conversating, then I heard the familiar chirp from his phone. I feel a pinch of jealousy. I once said that this love we share is intense and all-consuming as anything I've ever experienced. But every day and each time he walks out the door I wonder if I will ever possess it 100%. He is like a firefly so beautiful and hard to catch. So, I won't question him or go through his phone. I won't nag or stress him out. Sometimes I wonder if I deserve to be loved completely, wholeheartedly, unconditionally. DO I? Does he Really love me? I know I deserve somebody that wants me and me only. I can't play games with him anymore. It's been a long week; I wonder if he thinks there's anything good about me. SMH."

Francesca questioned her self-worth... *"I miss him! It's been four days since I've seen or heard from him and if I'm honest it's getting to me. I don't understand why I always have to play games or become someone I'm not just to make a point. Why can't he just see that I love him and we live happily ever after? It's hard."*

"As I sit here and write and cry and listen to music, I'm tired physically, mentally and emotionally. I just want to meet myself for the first time. Who am I supposed to be? The person I was always meant to be. Loving freely living purposefully. All the people I pushed away, I cry for today. "Today I am somewhere between the future and the past. Like standing at the top of a hill or being at the top of a roller coaster ... the hardest thing to do is to let go believing that what lies ahead is more promising than what's left behind."

In this statement Francesca was battling with herself about holding on to the relationship that she knew would end up a disaster because the signs were demonstrated daily right before her eyes and the uncertainty of a future that could be better if she would let go. Do you see red flags? Francesca's red flags weren't minor issues. They were deep personal betrayals that affected her emotionally. The flags you see please don't take it lightly, make excuses for, or dismiss them.

Here are some red flags that Francesca wrote about in her journal, which personally affected her:

1. **CHEATING AND DECEPTION** - One of the earliest red flags Francesca experienced was her partner's unfaithfulness. Cheating is not only a betrayal of trust but a clear indicator of disrespect and disregard for the relationship. Despite promises of change Francesca's partner continued to engage in infidelity, leading to a cycle of lies and emotional manipulation.

2. **INVOLVEMENT WITH MULTIPLE 'BABY MAMAS'** - Francesca found herself dealing with her partner's previous relationships, often involving the mothers of his other children. These dynamics led to conflict and created an atmosphere of competition, where Francesca often felt insecure and devalued, forced to compete for his attention and affection. Ladies don't take this lightly; it reinforces feelings of inadequacy and left Francesca constantly questioning her worth.

3. **MANIPULATIVE BEHAVIOR** - Francesca's partner was highly manipulative, using emotional tactics to control and confuse her. Manipulation comes in many forms such as guilt-tripping, gaslighting, or

making promises of change that never materialize. Francesca would leave a relationship and find herself being drawn back in, believing that things would improve, only to be hurt again. This form of emotional abuse made it hard for Francesca to leave the relationship. She felt as though she was responsible for fixing the problems or maybe overreacting.

4. **CONSTANT NEED FOR ATTENTION** - Francesca's partner had a constant need for attention, which was another red flag. He thrived on attention he received from others, often putting his own needs above her. This behavior is typically rooted in insecurity and a desire for validation, which led to toxic patterns where a person continually seeks out new sources of attention through affairs, public displays of power, or attention seeking behavior which undermine the relationship.

5. **POSSESSIVENESS AND CONTROL** - As the relationship progressed, Francesca's partner became more possessive and controlling. What might have initially seemed like concern or protectiveness quickly evolved into isolating behavior. He would monitor her movements, control who she interacted with and dictate her choices, all under the disguise of "love" or "protecting" her. Possessiveness is never a sign of love, it's a warning that a partner is seeking to exert control over your life. This kind of behavior can escalate quickly into more serious forms of emotional behavior and physical abuse.

6. **ABUSIVE AND BULLYING BEHAVIOR** - Francesca's partner became a bully, using intimidation, threats, and even physical aggression to keep in line. Don't allow anyone to cross that line. Bullying in relationships often stems from insecurity, where one partner feels the need to dominate the other in order to maintain power and control. This behavior left Francesca feeling trapped, fearful, and unsure of how to escape. The impact of being treated that way affected Francesca psychologically. It left her devastated, depressed, and with deep a sense of hopelessness.

7. **STREET INVOLVEMENT AND DANGEROUS ASSOCIATIONS** - Francesca's partner's involvement in street life and dangerous environments exposed Francesca to serious risks. His lifestyle put her in harm's way. Being tied to someone involved in illegal or dangerous

activities increases the likelihood of physical harm and further isolates the person from potential sources of help or support. Francesca was caught in a world she didn't belong to, struggling to reconcile her love for him with the dangerous reality of his actions.

8. **SEXUAL PERVERSION** - Francesca's partner also engaged in sexually manipulative and perverse behavior. Sexual perversion refers to any distortion of the purity of sex as God intended. When people seek sexual fulfillment outside the parameters of marriage, or when sex is twisted into something degrading or exploitative, it becomes perverse. Some examples of sexual perversion include *Fornication* - engaging in sexual activity outside marriage. Engaging in sex before marriage can lead to emotional and spiritual complications. When we give ourselves physically without the foundation of a committed marriage, it can create feelings of insecurity, guilt, and confusion. There will always be a question in your mind whether your relationship is based on love or lust. *Adultery* - infidelity within marriage, violating the trust and unity between spouses. Your body is the temple of the Lord and does not belong to you. Sexual relationships are deeply emotional, physical, and spiritual connections that were intended by God to be shared within the sacred boundaries of marriage between one man and one woman reflecting the covenantal relationship between Christ and his church.

These were signs she overlooked, hoping things would eventually change. But in the end, those red flags intensified, leading to deeper pain and heartbreak. The dangers of not taking heed to these warning signs can be life altering, as ignoring them may result in physical harm.

REFLECTION |

Dear Sisters,

I write to you with a heavy heart and a plead that I hope will prick your heart. My daughter, Francesca Harris-Scarborough, lost her life and the life of her unborn child due to domestic violence. Francesca was shot twice in the heart. My heart is so broken. No mother should have to bury her child, especially under these circumstances. No family should have to plan a funeral. I share out of my heart, not for pity, but out of urgency to take heed of the warning signs, to recognize the red flags that are so clearly displayed before your eyes and to protect yourselves. If you are in an abusive relationship, I plead with you to get out now.

My daughter was a beautiful young lady, filled with so much potential. She loved fiercely and like many, maybe even you, believed in second chances. Her love made her vulnerable to someone who didn't value her the way she deserved. In her journal she shared that she knew she was being mistreated and made excuses. She thought he was her project. She thought she could change him; she thought she could make him better. Ladies, he is not your project, you cannot change him, you can't make him better. When you leave, your life is not over, you will live again, you will love again. You are loved. Please know today, I love you with the love of a mother, sister, and friend.

If you find yourself questioning if your relationship is healthy, please, I beg you to leave. Cry Loud, Spare Not, Speak Up, you don't have to suffer in silence. Tell someone, get help. Call a domestic abuse hotline, find a shelter, take out a restraining order. Francesca promised me that she was going to get a restraining order, but she didn't make it. Please don't wait. Do it today, do it now. Like Francesca, if you wait it may be too late. More red Flags are listed in the resource section of this book.

With all my Heart,

Shirley H. Scarborough

MY PRAYER FOR YOU

Father in the name of Jesus,

We come to you today with open hearts, standing in the gap on behalf of every woman who may be struggling, who may feel trapped, who may be questioning if she is safe in her relationship. Lord, open their eyes that they may see clearly and open their hearts that will take heed to the red flags you show them. Let them feel your presence, your power today. Help them to know their worth, Lord. Remind them that they are deeply valued and loved and are deserving of love.

Father we pray that you would give them a spirit of courage. Give them the strength to face their fears, to recognize any harm they may be enduring. Move out shame or hesitation that may hold them back. Let them know that you are a certainty during this uncertain time. Replace doubt with assurance.

Lord, we pray against every spirit of fear. Remind each woman of your word that you have not given her a spirit of fear, but power, love and a sound mind. Break any chains of intimidation, fear, manipulation that hold her back. Loose the warring angels Michael and Gabriel to go before her and protect her from hurt, harm and danger. Keep their minds in perfect peace, supply their every need.

Father, let them feel your love, real love, an unconditional and agape love. Cover every lady with your blood. We thank you Lord.

In The Name of Jesus,

Amen

CELEBRATE YOUR BIG WINS

LET GO OF NEGATIVE THOUGHTS
FIND A MOMENT OF PEACE
PRACTICE GRATITUDE
PRACTICE SELF LOVE
SET BOUNDARIES

_____
_____
_____
_____
_____
_____
_____
_____
_____
_____
_____
_____
_____
_____
_____

___ / ___ / ___

Make a copy of this page to
continuously celebrate your wins
day after day!

TAKE A BREAK
FORGIVE YOURSELF
CHOOSE SELF CARE
SHARE YOUR STORY
ASK FOR HELP

CHAPTER
Nine

LONGING FOR LOVE | HER SILENT STRUGGLE

SHATTERED BUT NOT DESTROYED

Dear Journal

> 66
>
> Why can't he see that I love him and we live happily ever after.
>
> 99

Francesca

9 Chapter
LONGING FOR LOVE | HER SILENT STRUGGLE

I n her own words, she once wrote in her journal:

"Dear Journal,
I am in love with love. I always have been, always waiting on my prince charming to live happily ever after with. Maybe it's just foolish. Maybe it's childish. Sometimes I wonder if I deserve to be loved completely, wholeheartedly, unconditionally. DO I? Does he really love me? I know I deserve somebody that wants me and me only. I can't play games with him anymore. It hurts so badly. Worse than a bee sting, worse than a gunshot. THIS TIME HE WILL SHOW ME AND IF HE DOESN'T, I'LL KNOW IT WASN'T REAL."

Francesca's journal reflects what many of us experience, the yearning for someone to come into our lives and make everything better. She spent many years waiting for love to fix what was broken inside, much like Sleeping Beauty waiting for that one kiss to change her world.

In the first sentence, Franny states, *"I AM IN LOVE WITH LOVE..."* She wasn't just in love with a person; she was in love with the idea of love itself. This yearning was shaped by emotional, psychological, societal factors, and childhood traumas. As a mother with a heart broken by the loss of my daughter, who was tragically murdered while in an abusive relationship, I urge you to reflect on these questions because I don't want anyone else to suffer as Francesca did, holding onto a fantasy that never led to the safety or happiness she deserved.

I ask you the following: Are you in love with love? Are you in love with the fantasy of being in love? Is there a Francesca in your house? Is there someone in your life, perhaps yourself, who is waiting for love to make everything better? Did you ever experience feelings of abandonment or rejection in childhood? Holding on to the idea of love can be powerful, but when it's based on the fantasy of being saved, it can be dangerous. Love shouldn't be about rescue; it should be about mutual respect, care and understanding. Real love begins within. Everyone is worthy of love, but it's important to recognize that no one person can fill every void.

For Francesca, the fantasy of being in love with love became a coping mechanism for the pain of separation from her parents. When her family separated, Francesca didn't adjust well, she was deeply disappointed and grieved the loss. She would say, *"my dad (her birth father) is coming back."* It's ironic to me that, Franny never mentioned her birth mother coming back to get her, but she held her birth father accountable for returning, as well as for satisfying the deep seeded need to feel loved, cared for and wanted. He never returned.

This unmet need created a wound that she carried into her teenage and adult years. For many girls, this longing for love often manifests in different ways: through promiscuity, rebellion, substance abuse, low self-esteem, and negative behavior problems. If a daughter doesn't feel loved or wanted as a child, the need for validation and attention grows deeper and more desperate, often carrying over into adulthood.

It is very important that, if at all possible, the father takes his role as dad, loving his daughter, spending time with her, being available for her. He needs to be the first man to validate her, send her flowers, and open the door for her. She needs to witness him opening the door for her mother. Through her father validating her, she sees her dad as a hero, this is how she will know how to be treated in marriage or in a relationship. Many times, fathers forget the girls and leave them to the mother because the girls don't throw footballs. Sometimes the daughter may get a father and daughter dance once a year. This is not enough. Daughters need security, consistency, she needs to understand what it feels like to lay in her dad's arms, to feel his strong shoulders that says everything is ok. If it affects you, it will reflect through you, through your behavior.

When Franny's birth father didn't come back to get her, her heart was broken, her worth was devalued. This opened up a gaping wound. In the natural, an open wound that is not treated will likely have bacteria to set in.

Just as our skin covers our organs, our father and mother are our protection, the shield that God has placed over us. This shield begins from the moment of conception. The fetus is alive and its skin can be broken. Words have power, so we need to be mindful of what we say, because what we say can also cause deep wounds. When a parent expresses a desire to not have a child, considers the child a mistake, discusses getting an abortion, or feels unhappy or disappointed about the child's gender, regardless of the reason, the skin is broken and it can spiritually create an opening for unclean spirits. This can be likened to an infected wound, inviting in feelings of rejection and abandonment.

What is your rejection? You may feel like you're not pretty enough, or that you're the black sheep in the family. Perhaps you feel inadequate or not smart enough, or maybe you feel like the clumsy child. It's possible that you resemble a parent, and they may be in a strained relationship with the other parent. Maybe you felt as though your parents favored a sibling over you, or maybe you feel like your skin color is too dark or too light, or your hair texture is different from your siblings, or you feel too fat or too skinny. These are examples of what causes feelings of rejection, and they impact individuals of all ages and backgrounds. It's crucial to recognize and address these feelings.

Franny dealt with rejection and abandonment from events that occurred in her early years before coming to my house. Unresolved rejection can cause a person to build emotional walls to protect themselves from further hurt. When this rejection is not addressed, the emotional wound deepens over time, leading to a fear of rejection that takes root within the soul. As a result, we may find ourselves living on the edge, unable to fully trust others, receive love, and limiting our own capacity to love in return. This lack of trust cheats us out of genuine love. We may also develop a need for attention, approval, and may overcompensate through our appearance (short dresses, revealing clothing, etc.), body modifications (implants, injections, multiple tattoos and piercings), and other means. It's a cry on the inside, "Can you see me?" This is an internal cry for recognition and acceptance. However, the more we try to fill this void, the emptier we feel. This can lead to a continuous cycle of feeling the need to do more.

Francesca's journal entry went on to reveal the deep emotional turmoil and the yearning she carried within her. "*I have always been waiting on my prince charming to live happily ever after with. Maybe it's just foolish, maybe it's childish...*" These words reflect a longing we can relate to, a desire for a love that is pure, unwavering and perfect. This love does *not* exist. I will be married forty-five years and have yet to experience that. Francesca admits to holding onto a vision of love that promises a happily ever after, but even she doubts its existence. The self-awareness in her words, "maybe it's just foolish, maybe it's childish," shows that she understood that real love is more complex than the fantasy she was holding onto.

"*Sometimes I wonder if I deserve to be loved completely, wholeheartedly, unconditionally...*" This sentence captures Francesca's deep insecurity and self-doubt. She questioned her worthiness, wondering if she truly deserved the kind of love she desired. Her use of the word "unconditionally" is highlighting her need for a love without limits, without conditions or expectations, something she never fully received or allowed herself to receive. Francesca's soul was fragmented, scattered.

What does a fragmented or scattered soul look like? What is the soul? The soul is often described as the very essence of who we are —the core of our being that defines our identity, emotions, and deepest desires. It's what connects us to God and others, guiding our moral compass and giving us purpose. But what happens when our soul becomes fragmented or scattered? A fragmented soul is one that has been broken, divided, or torn apart by life's circumstances. This fragmentation can happen due to trauma, betrayal, prolonged grief, or the pursuit of unhealthy relationships and patterns. When our soul is scattered, we feel disconnected from ourselves, from others, and from God. It's as though pieces of us have been left in the hands of others or trapped in past experiences, leaving us feeling incomplete and adrift.

The soul is the seat of our emotions, thoughts, and spirit. It's what gives us life and allows us to experience joy, pain, love, and connection. In many religious and spiritual traditions, the soul is eternal, reflecting the image of God and connecting us to Him. It carries our identity and purpose, influencing how we engage with the world and those around us. In the Bible, the soul is often seen as our inner being, the part of us that desires communion with God. Psalm 23 speaks of the Lord restoring our soul, highlighting the need for healing and wholeness when we've become broken or lost. Ask God to restore your soul.

A fragmented soul often manifests itself in ways that affect our mental, emotional, and spiritual health.

Some signs include:

1. **Emotional Instability:** A fragmented soul can leave you feeling overwhelmed by your emotions. You may swing between joy and despair, unable to find a balance. Anxiety, depression, and a constant sense of unease can become daily companions.

2. **Lack of Purpose or Direction:** When the soul is scattered, it's hard to find direction in life. You may feel lost, unsure of your purpose, and unable to connect with what once brought you meaning.

3. **Relational Disconnection:** A fragmented soul struggles to build and maintain healthy relationships. You might push people away, isolate yourself, or be drawn to relationships that aren't good for you. Trust issues, fear of abandonment, or an inability to be vulnerable are common.

4. **Spiritual Disconnection:** Feeling distant from God or spiritually numb can be a sign of a fragmented soul. You might feel as though God is far away or that you're unable to connect with Him in prayer or worship.

5. **Repeating Harmful Patterns:** A scattered soul often falls into cycles of self-destructive behavior. Whether it's unhealthy relationships, addiction, or emotional dependence, the soul may seek comfort in things that only bring more fragmentation.

If you find that your soul is fragmented or scattered, healing is possible. Just as God is the healer of our physical wounds, He can also mend the fractures in our soul. The process requires intentional steps toward wholeness, including:

1. **Surrendering to God:** Acknowledge that healing comes through God's grace and love. Opening your heart to Him allows for the restoration of the soul.

2. **Letting Go of the Past:** Healing often involves releasing past traumas, hurts, and disappointments. This may mean forgiving others, forgiving yourself, or simply letting go of the expectations that caused you pain.

3. **Reconnecting Spiritually:** Spend time in prayer, meditation, and scripture. Rebuilding your spiritual connection will help ground you and restore a sense of purpose.

4. **Seeking Healthy Relationships:** Surround yourself with people who nurture and support your soul. Build relationships that are based on trust, respect, and mutual care.

5. **Self-Care and Reflection:** Take time to care for your emotional and mental health. Journaling, therapy, or spiritual counseling can be vital tools in understanding the areas of your soul that need healing.

A whole and healed soul is one that radiates peace, purpose, and connection. Though life may scatter you, God is always ready to bring the pieces back together, restoring you to wholeness and filling you with His love and grace.

"Does he really love me?"

Francesca's self-worth was tied to being loved by someone else. Her questioning reveals a deep uncertainty about her relationship and whether she was truly valued and cherished as she longed to be. Francesca longed for validation, for someone who would see her as worthy of love just as she was.

"I know I deserve someone that wants me and me only..."

Here, Francesca asserts her need for exclusivity, for a love that is focused solely on her. This shows how deeply she wanted to feel chosen, to be first priority, after years of feeling secondary or abandoned. She was tired of feeling like an option, tired of playing games in love. Francesca no longer wanted to play these games in love. She was not tolerating halfhearted affection. *"I can't play games with him anymore..."* At this point, Francesca was exhausted. She was tired of the emotional roller coasters in this relationship, tired of the manipulation, the uncertainty, and the constant betrayal. Love wasn't supposed to feel like this. It was never supposed to be painful. In her heart, love was meant to be a dream like the fairy tale of kissing the handsome prince and living happily ever after. But when Francesca woke up, the dream had soured into a nightmare. Instead of a prince, she found herself kissing an ugly frog. The fantasy of love, once so enchanting, had become a harsh reality that only brought cycles of hurt and disappointment.

"It hurts so bad, more than a bee sting, more than a gunshot..."

It really hurt my heart to read Francesca's analogy, especially when she compared her emotion to a gunshot, because she died with two gunshots to her heart. The tragic irony of her words is almost unbearable. I can understand a bee sting. A bee string is sharp, sudden and surprising. It's a quick stinging pain that lingers but is bearable. It's like finding out he cheated on you. A bee sting might have hurt for a moment, put ointment on it, the swelling goes away, and the pain gets better. She had never been physically shot at the time, yet she chose to describe her emotional suffering in such a violent, devastating way, as if foreshadowing her own fate. It's heartbreaking to me to think that her deepest pain felt so severe that only a gunshot could capture the intensity of what she was going through. Even though it's years later, she died of a wounded heart and a wound in the heart.

Do you find yourself carrying these feelings into your adult relationships, waiting for someone to fix you, to save you? What was broken in your past? Franny carried her fears into the future, through the spirit of self-rejection. Self-Rejection is a form of self-sabotage. It occurs when a person convinces themself that they are not enough and sees themself as a failure. They operate out of fear, fearing failure even when they are already succeeding. This person convinces themself to quit while ahead or not even try. They are quick to encourage others about their success and to use their gifts, but they don't do the same for themself. They think they're not worthy, compare themself and their abilities to others, which causes them not to succeed. They settle for less and give less when they have so much to offer. They're afraid of being rejected and are always worried about what the other person thinks, which makes them change their goals and dreams. They are people pleasers and don't walk in the peace of God. They are inconsistent, and cannot endure in relationships. They lack confidence and feel as though they don't matter.

"If he doesn't, I'll know it wasn't real…"

Francesca was testing the authenticity of the love she was receiving. She questioned whether the person she loved truly cared for her or whether she was once again being deceived. The emotional toll of trying to turn a frog into a prince, trying to fit him into a fantasy he could never live up to, was draining.

This journal entry paints a picture of a woman who desperately wanted to be loved but was caught between the fantasy of love and the harsh reality of her relationships. Francesca's emotional wounds ran deep, stemming from abandonment and rejection, and they shaped her expectations of love. She lined up for a fairy tale ending but was coming to terms with the fact that love, in reality, is often far more painful and complicated than the stories she clung to. Her words are a cry for help, a cry for love she felt she deserved but never fully received, and a cry for the peace and security she so desperately needed. Francesca's words are a powerful reminder of the dangers of holding onto fantasies of love that don't exist in reality.

Are there signs or red flags in your relationships that you may be overlooking? Are you ignoring unhealthy patterns while chasing after a fairytale ending?

Franny kept finding herself in the same type of relationships, choosing guys with the same characteristics with different names. Everyone she had a relationship with became her project. She felt like she could fix them and design them just for her. Franny spent her time waiting and looking for love, she would meet them and they would leave. She questioned why every guy she was in a relationship with left her or ended up in jail.

"Dear Journal...
I miss him! It's been four days since I've seen or heard from him and if I'm honest it's getting to me. I don't understand why I always have to play games or become someone I'm not just to make a point. Why can't he just see that I love him and we live happily ever after? It's hard."

She started out feeling safe in his arms, while he showered her with gifts, taking care of her needs and at the same time he was sizing her up, testing her, learning her strengths and weaknesses. In the beginning he was patient and very kind but calculated.

Are you waiting for love to save you, just like Francesca did? Do you find yourself clinging to the fantasy of love, believing that when the right person comes along, all the pieces of your life will suddenly fit together?

Francesca, like many of us, was in love with the idea of love, believing that it would fix everything. But the truth is, no person can save us from our pain. Waiting for someone else to fill the void can blind us to the reality of toxic relationships and make it harder to see the danger ahead.

What might happen if you stopped waiting and faced the reality of love and life, beyond the fairytale? What steps can you take to build a love that's built on mutual respect, effort, and seeing each other's worth, instead of waiting for a fairy tale?

Have you ever imagined that once you find "the one," everything will fall into place, just like a princess waiting for her fate to be changed by someone else? Francesca writes and dreams about her Prince Charming coming to swoop in and bring her happiness. But real life doesn't work that way, does it?

Developing healthy, realistic relationships both with oneself and with others is essential for long term well-being and happiness. While the idea of fantasy relationships can be strong, genuine and lasting connections are built on trust, respect, and open communication.

Healthy relationships involve seeing both oneself and others as they truly are without the filter of romanticized or idealized notions.

Fortunately, there are many resources and professional support systems available to help individuals move beyond the romanticized ideas of love and build strong, healthy relationships.

The greatest resource we can consult is the Bible. The Bible offers insights into personal growth/development and the qualities of love, but also provides clear guidance on the importance of respect, commitment and honoring one another in romantic relationships. For those seeking romantic or marriage relationships, the Bible emphasizes the significance of marriage as a covenant that precedes sexual intimacy, underscoring the sacredness and commitment involved. The Biblical ideal of marriage is often presented as a committed, life-long partnership where love and mutual respect can flourish. 1 Corinthians 13, describes real love and the characteristics of love. God is love and He loves you.

Life and relationship coaches are another resource. This resource guides individuals in setting personal goals, building self-confidence, and developing the skills needed to navigate dating. Practical advice on relationship dynamics and communication skills.

For those that prefer more structured learning, online courses and workshops provide insights into healthy relationships, communication, and emotional intelligence.

Educational websites offer articles, videos, and quizzes focused on building healthy relationships. Relationship apps provide users with relationship coaching, lessons and exercises. Therapists and counselors can help individuals explore their own relationship patterns, address self-worth, and set boundaries. Couples therapy is available for those already in a relationship. Couples therapy provides a safe space to communicate openly, resolve conflict, and build stronger foundations. It helps couples to understand each other's needs and build a realistic vision of love.

There are many more resources such as books, journals, guided workbooks on self-love, support groups that deal with fantasy, podcasts and channels by relationship experts.

Whether seeking support for oneself or guiding someone else, these resources can provide active advice, self-awareness tools and skills needed to build meaningful, healthy relationships grounded in reality.

HEART MENDER |
LONGING FOR LOVE: HER SILENT STRUGGLE

Father in the name of Jesus,

I lift up every woman that is reading this book to you, the One who knows her heart in its fullness, even the parts hidden by silence and tears. Lord, you see her pain, her deep longing to be loved, cherished, validated and understood. You know the cries within her heart, the ache she carries quietly.

Lord, wrap her in your arms and let her feel the warmth of your presence, of your unconditional love. Remind her that your love is constant, pure, and healing. Remind her that she is the apple of your eye and that she is fearfully and wonderfully made. Let her know that she is your masterpiece, that she is a designer's original. Help her to see herself as you see her, complete and worthy of love.

Let her know that she is never alone and that you are with her always.

Father, fill the empty places within her with your peace. Reveal the plans that you have for her in your timing.

Father, bring people into her life who will honor her heart, uplift her spirit, recognize the beauty within her, and celebrate her presence.

Renew her hope, Lord, and help her to find joy in the waiting. Let her know that your love is more than enough to fill her heart completely and that your plans are good even when she can't see or understand them.

In your precious name I pray,

Amen

CHAPTER *Ten*

UNSPOKEN WORDS | THERE'S GOOD IN GOODBYE

SHATTERED BUT NOT DESTROYED

Dear Journal

> "
>
> OMG. It's one of those days. I can't put into words how I feel right now.
>
> "

Francesca

10 Chapter
UNSPOKEN WORDS | THERE'S GOOD IN GOODBYE

I recently found a letter written to me by Francesca. I don't know when she wrote it, but this is the first time I've ever read it. Her words are filled with raw emotion, honesty, and the kind of vulnerability that breaks my heart. In this letter, she tried to share with me the things she never said out loud, and now, I want to respond. I want her to know what I couldn't tell her while she was alive. I want to incorporate her words with the things I hope she knew before she was taken from me.

The loss of a child is an indescribable pain, a grief that forever changes the mother left behind. For those who face the sudden and unexpected death of a child, the grief is often mixed with countless unspoken words and unanswered questions that remain in our heart. The weight of those unsaid words lingers.

Francesca wrote, *"Mom, I have never been so upfront with you as I am about to be now. I only want you to understand where I'm coming from and not jump to conclusions. First, let me start by saying that from day one, you treated me excellently. I could never say anything contrary to that because it is the truth. I know I haven't always acted like it. Maybe with my actions, but I know that you have always had my back, no matter what, and I appreciate it. You were always there for me, even when I wasn't upfront with stuff."*

I hope she knew before she was taken from me that no matter how distant she may have felt at times, I was always ready to be there for her. I knew she was struggling to find her way, and any distance that may have been there didn't change my love for her. I hope she really knew that I was always praying for her and that my love for her was unconditional and unwavering. I hope she really knew the love in my heart for her.

"Mom, please don't give up on me. I need you and never realized how much of a backbone you were for me. I feel so empty. I don't understand my

purpose. I don't want to fail. I want to know love. I know you love me, but I don't know how to love myself."

I hope she knew I never gave up on her, there were times when I didn't have the answers to her hurts and disappointments, but I hope she knew that when she felt lost, I was trying to be her anchor. I hope she knew that she was my heart and no matter what she was going through I was going to see her through, I hope she knew that I never let go of the hope that she would find her way through the darkness. I hope she knew how to know love on her own. I hope she knew she had mine and I hope she knew through my actions just how deeply I loved her.

"There are so many things going on in my head that hold me down. I used to think I was smart, but now I'm doubting myself. Sometimes I feel like I'm not good enough. I feel like everyone is better than me at everything. You probably think I should get over my situation, but it's easier for some people than others. I need answers."

I hope she knew that she was special, that she was smart, beautiful, and capable in ways she couldn't always see. I hope she knew that I saw her strength, even when she couldn't feel it. I hope she knew that I would've moved mountains to help her find peace. I hope she knew before she took her last breath, that I was proud of her. I hope she knew that I saw her beauty, not just on the outside but within her.

"Sometimes I'm afraid. I always wanted to be grown, and now I'm afraid of growing up. I don't know what's wrong with me. I'm scared of responsibilities. I have lots of fears. Sometimes I dream of dying. I dream of people shooting me or stabbing me. I am scared to death to die. I'm really sorry for everything, Mom, for acting crazy."

I hope she knew that I never saw her as a burden, that I didn't think she was crazy. I hope she knew that I understood her fears and failures. I hope she knew I imparted everything I was capable of. I hope she knew that she was validated by me. I hope she knew I did my best to give her the best. I hope she knew I forgave her, the choices she made in life that caused me hurt, disappointment and grief.

I hope she knew I would always carry her with me. That in my heart she is alive, her laughter, her tears, her dreams and even her struggles. Before

93

Francesca's sudden death, I hope she knew how deeply she was loved, not just in fleeting moments, but in every breath, every prayer, and every thought. I hope she knew my love was unconditional, eternal, and unwavering. I hope she understood that no matter what disagreements, misunderstandings, or mistakes, my heart was always open to her. I hope she knew the depth of my love, and that my love extended beyond words, beyond actions.

I hope she knew I was proud of the woman that she was becoming even in the midst of her challenges. Life wasn't easy for Francesca, and there were times she made choices that broke my heart. But I was proud of her resilience, her spirit and the way she fought to navigate a world that didn't always show the love and care she deserved. I hope she knew I recognized her efforts, that I saw her trying and that my disappointment was never in her as a person, but in the circumstances that surrounded her.

I hope she knew that I would have done anything I could to protect her. I hope she knew I was always on her side, even when I couldn't fix everything. I hope she knew that the motherly advice, the reprimands I gave, were to shield her from the hurt, abuse, and dangers in this world.

I hope she knew that she was enough, that I believed in her, that my heart was connected to hers, that I had her at best interest at heart. I never got to say goodbye. I never had the chance to tell her how much she meant to me in those final moments. There are a million things I would have said, words of comfort, of love, or forgiveness, and of hope. I would have made sure that she knew her life mattered and that her story wasn't just about pain and loss but about love, family, and all the moments we shared.

I hope she knew no matter what, she will always be my daughter and no amount of time or tragedy can take that away. Francesca wrote *"Thank God for the good in goodbye"*. When I read this, I felt as though this was God's way of loving me. I couldn't find the peace I needed because there was no closure in Francesca's death. No one has been held accountable for taking her life or the life of the son she was carrying. The grief is immense, and at first, it seemed impossible to find peace or closure in her death. The Lord began to show me the good in saying goodbye to her. Getting to this point in my grieving is unreal for me. This phrase was as though Francesca spoke it to me to help me heal.

This book is a way of saying goodbye, to raise awareness against domestic abuse, to help a young lady that's saying she is not smart enough, pretty enough. Yes, my heart is truly broken but there is some good in goodbye, Francesca.

IN MEMORY OF
YOUR LOVED ONE

WRITE A LETTER IN MEMORY OF YOUR LOVED ONE

What do you wish you had done or said? What do you hope they knew?

_____

_____

_____

_____

_____

_____

_____

_____

_____

_____

_____

_____

_____

_____

_____

_____

_____

_____

_____

_____

CHAPTER
Eleven

A MOTHER'S CRY | TURNING PAIN INTO POWER

SHATTERED BUT NOT DESTROYED

Dear Journal

> 66
>
> Everyday is a struggle and I'm constantly having to put things into perspective.
>
> 99

Francesca

11 *Chapter*

A MOTHER'S CRY | TURNING PAIN INTO POWER

In the weeks and months following Francesca's death, my heart was grieving so deeply I didn't know how I would manage it. Grief became an all-consuming weight, one that felt unbearable at times. I was weeping, my heart heavy with an intensity I can barely describe. I wept for Francesca, my daughter, whose life was stolen. I wept for the decision she made that led her into darkness and for the way she settled for less than she deserved. I wept for the murderer - someone so lost that they could commit such a violent act. But my tears were not just for my daughter or her killer. I wept for every woman who has never experienced the love of a father or mother, or who has never truly known love in her life. I wept for the woman who has never felt validated, who struggles to recognize her own worth. I cried for the abused woman, worn down by emotional, mental, and physical torment until it feels like a normal part of life. My heart ached for those who feel trapped in a cycle of believing they're unworthy of better days ahead. I mourned for the woman who sees dreaming or hoping for something greater as a curse. I wept for the one who endures insults, humiliation, and disrespect, convinced that no one else would ever want her. I grieved for the woman whose only goal is to make it through each day, surviving one breath at a time. I felt for those facing mental illness, those fighting against addiction, and for the suicidal woman who can't see the light at the end of her tunnel. My heart broke for those oppressed and caught in cycles of depression, lost in their own pain.

I always keep a notepad by my bedside, and on one particularly difficult night while I was deep in grief, I fell asleep with tears still in my eyes. In that pain-filled slumber, I had a vision: the ground began to crack open, and a microphone emerged from the earth. I found myself writing repeatedly in my notepad, "*Not in vain.*" Her death would not be in vain. I also scribbled down, "*Cry loud and spare not.*" There would be beauty for ashes, and everything would ultimately bring God glory. My daughter may be gone, but she will never be forgotten. Death is not the end of her story. I am determined that Francesca's legacy will endure; her memory will live on, and she will rise again. No force on earth can keep her down. I refuse to let grief control me, define me, or destroy my life. While I can't change what happened to my daughter, I am committed to being her voice. Through her death, I believe many women will live.

From that moment on, my nightly notes turned into an outcry—a fervent plea for justice, healing, and hope. My mission and assignment became crystal clear: to empower both young and older women to understand who they are and whose they are. *Cry Loud, Spare Not, Speak Up, Inc.,* a 501(c)(3) nonprofit organization, was founded with a mission to empower and uplift women and girls impacted by domestic violence and abusive relationships, in memory of Francesca Harris-Scarborough. We aim to provide education, mentoring, and resources encouraging women to find their voice and embrace self-worth through self-confidence, self-love, and self-esteem. By starting my non-profit, *Cry Loud*, it allowed me to turn my pain into power and ensure that her death will not be in vain by helping to educate, advocate, and support other women and girls in domestic abuse relationships. *Cry Loud* fosters a safe environment where women and girls will value their self-worth, learn to love themselves, learn to develop healthy relationships, and set healthy boundaries. We are committed to spreading awareness, prevention, advocating for an end to domestic violence, and committing it all for God's glory. We visualize a world where every woman and girl know their inherent value and is empowered to break free from abusive relationships. Above all, I want them to know that Jesus loves them unconditionally.

As I sit here and reflect on my journey since Franny's death, the pain of losing my daughter is a constant thought, but I've managed to transform the pain into a powerful means for change. What began as an outlet for my grief has very quickly evolved into something much more significant: a lifeline for women and girls trapped in abusive relationships. My call for change is both a personal and passionate plea. I challenge each person reading this to confront the epidemic of domestic violence. This isn't just a "women's issue," it's a pivotal human issue. Every woman enduring silent suffering and every girl who believes abuse is her destiny must know she is not alone and that there is real hope and a way out.

Hope is truly attainable when each of us acknowledges and engages in actions that are bold, purposeful, and life changing. We cannot afford to stand by passively, ignoring the signs, like black eyes, bruises, isolation, personality changes, or lower self-esteem. Nor should we think that it's someone else's problem. It's time to stop pretending we're okay, believing that an abuser will change, or accepting that it's our fault. We must break free from hiding our pain behind forced smiles. We need to raise our voices louder than the silence that abuse thrives in. Seeking help from trusted friends, family members, or advocates is essential. We must leave at the first sign of abuse—there is no time to waste. Acknowledging and overcoming the fear and anxiety of leaving is part of the process; but having a safe exit plan is crucial. We are far braver than we realize. We must trust that God is in control. His unwavering love for us remains, and He has not changed His mind about you.

This journey is leading me on a clearer path toward healing and empowerment. The memories of Franny and my unrelenting faith and trust in God provide me the strength to move forward, and yes—the strength to forgive the person who took my daughter's life. Forgiveness is not a sign of weakness, but a source of freedom. It doesn't mean forgetting, but it means reclaiming the power that was stolen from us. I want you to walk this road with me, as we uncover the strength within us to heal, empower, and ultimately, forgive.

I AM ENOUGH, I KNOW MY WORTH

These are excerpts from Francesca's journal:

"I used to think I was smart, but I started doubting myself and now I don't care. Sometimes I feel like I'm nothing, sometimes like any and everybody is better than me @ everything. I hate my body, and at times I feel used. There are so many things going on in my head that hold me down."

When we hear the word "worth" in everyday life, it is often equated with financial success or material achievements. Society is quick to define value by material achievements. News reports may talk about a celebrity's worth in terms of dollars, but I beg to differ. A true worth cannot be defined by society's standards. A woman's worth goes far beyond these measures; it is defined by God, who has uniquely crafted her with purpose, intention, and love.

Francesca's words echo the struggle many feel when they don't see their worth reflected in the world around us. Ephesians 2:10 [NIV] says, *"For we are his workmanship, created in Christ Jesus unto good works, which God hath before ordained that we should walk in them."* This verse speaks directly to our worth and purpose, reminding us that each of us is God's own masterpiece, intentionally and uniquely crafted. The word workmanship in Greek means poiema, which means poem. Imagine being God's poiema, God's poem. God took some dirt and created us to be His workmanship. You are God's masterpiece. God's Creation, and He's not ashamed of you. Before the foundation of the world God knew and ordained your victories, your downfalls, your setbacks, and your failure. Today, release yourself. Stop holding yourself hostage. Stop believing the lies the devil tells you about you.

Make it personal and say that I am God's handiwork, I am God's masterpiece. God is the artist. When God created you, he detailed every part of you. Your big lips, wide hips, wide nose, six toes, nappy hair, light skin or dark skin. God made you unique, He designed you with His own hand with purpose, for a purpose and on purpose. Please know that you are not a mistake. And your mistakes don't define you, your mistakes are lessons to be learned so that you can go to the next level. You are a designer's original, one of a kind. No one has your fingerprints, your DNA. There are no duplicates. God made you just right. Before the foundation of the world, before He formed you in the womb, God knew your name before your parents named you. He called you and set you apart, He sanctified you.

Proverbs 23:7 [KJV] says, *"For as he thinketh in his heart, so is he...*" This means that a man is literally what he thinks, his character becomes the complete sum of all his thoughts with the thoughts shaping his life. When you invest in your thoughts it becomes an action. If you think of yourself in a negative manner, what you think will manifest. What do you think of you? If I think myself to be a failure, then I will fail. If you think yourself to never complete anything, you will begin many tasks but never completing any of them.

What are you saying or thinking about yourself? Speak life over you, speak positive things over you, speak the Word of God over you. I think myself to be the head and not the tail, the lender and not the borrower, the first and not the last. I think myself to have the favor of God because I am the apple of God's eye. I think myself to be happy, I think myself with all the flaws that the world has labeled me with, to be fearfully and wonderfully made. I think myself to be an overcomer, more than a conqueror because I can do all thing through Christ that strengthens me. I think myself to be more than enough, to be a woman of God, a woman of purpose, and a woman of value. My current situation is not my final destination. Where you are now is not where you're going. God loves you and God has plans for you to succeed and not to fail. God's love is perfect, and perfect love casts out all fear and doubt. I pray this book help you to find strength.

Turning pain into power has not been easy. This journey was not one that I asked for, but I am determined to honor God, my child's life, and those around me that still need help.

I am turning this pain into purpose. I created the non-profit, *Cry Loud Spare Not Speak Up, Inc.* Through my organization, I am hoping to:

1. Bring light to the signs of domestic violence, especially to young people. Through Cry Loud, we will educate, advocate, and support other women and girls in domestic abuse relationships. If I am able to save one life, my child's death was not in vain.
2. Encourage grieving parents. Grieve in your own time but find power/purpose to propel your loved one's memory. You could not prevent the circumstances, but you can decide on how to use the pain to stop another parent from grieving.

REFLECTION |
"I AM ENOUGH"

Take this opportunity to celebrate yourself, because you are worthy of love and appreciation just as you are. You possess a unique beauty that is not defined by societal standards or trends. Remember that your worth is not dependent on the opinions of others. Reflect on your strengths and talents. Celebrate all the victories in your life, whether it's something you've achieved or simply getting through a tough day.

Look in the mirror and acknowledge the person staring back—the unique, beautiful, wonderfully made individual, God's Masterpiece, who deserves love and respect.

LOVE LETTER TO MYSELF

_____,

_____

_____

_____

_____

_____

_____

_____

_____

_____

_____

_____

_____

_____

_____

_____

_____

_____

_____

_____

_____

CHAPTER
Twelve

IS THERE A FRANCESCA IN YOUR HOME?

SHATTERED BUT NOT DESTROYED

Dear Journal

"

It was always there, beneath the surface a treasure chest and it contained the tools I needed so many questions and no answers.

"

Francesca

12 Chapter
IS THERE A FRANCESCA IN YOUR HOME?

As parents, our foremost duty is to protect our children, going to great lengths to ensure their safety and provision. Often, we try to make up for what we lacked in our own childhoods, hoping our children will make better choices. Yet, in our attempts, we might sometimes become enablers, creating a world where our children believe all revolves around them, only to later confront a world that can be overwhelming and harsh.

Francesca's story mirrors this struggle. Her upbringing, marred by rejection, compels us to overcompensate for what she lacked. When she called me "mom," it felt like a breakthrough—a joy indescribable, yet intertwined with the challenge of guiding her through rejection. Francesca craves love much like a child seeking acceptance at any cost, unaware of the steep price it demands.

Every child, including those like Francesca, needs love that is boundary-defined. Unhealed wounds often prompt us to conform to others' needs, becoming vulnerable to exploitation. As parents, we can often see this in others' lives, but when faced with it at home, we feel like lost children ourselves, unsure how to guide.

Blessed with talent and a loving heart, Francesca's love became her Achilles' heel—the same love that could heal also causes harm. Love masked her pain, fueled self-sabotage and made her vulnerable. It caused her to redefine love through abuse, masking reality with desire.

Do you have a Francesca in your home? A child full of potential yet drowning in rejection, rebellion, and the false belief of knowing more than you? Such a child can become a stranger before your eyes, clutching at illusions, leaving you feeling powerless in the face of their choices.

As parents, we often feel burdened by unspoken words, watching as our children retreat into solitude with digital devices that foster illusions. Each retreat feels like a defeat, reminding us of an ache that grows with each rebellious choice and a sense of helplessness as they drift further from the guidance we offer.

But Francesca was also a woman who gave her best to those who deserved it the least, unaware of her own worth. She was the one who stayed for the long haul, quietly enduring lack and seeking love without limits. Her heart led her, often into toxic environments she found hard to leave. She risked everything, bearing responsibility for others' recklessness, seldom receiving anything in return. Though she knew better, she feels trapped, fearing that the meager love she received was the best she would ever have. Her smiles and laughter often masked her pain, while her soul, worn and weary, searched for validation in others, performing for love.

For mothers, compassion is key. Dealing with your child with empathy, understanding their world, and setting healthy boundaries is crucial. Establishing a space where they can freely express themselves without fear of judgment goes a long way. Manage your mental health and remember, it's not your fault. Encourage therapeutic support if needed and embrace patience, knowing that healing is a journey, not a race.

Francesca's advice to herself and others was to recognize self-worth and refuse to accept rejection. Embrace transparency and seek healing through therapy, prayer, and supportive networks. Pay attention to red flags and understand that love is secure, not abusive. Never accept being a secret—your value is immeasurable. Trust in God's divine guidance for choosing companions, and remember that each new day offers a chance to do better.

Whether you're the mother of a Francesca or a Francesca yourself, know there is hope. Embrace the healing process and invest in yourself as the most valuable project. You are resilient, and you will not only survive but thrive.

CHAPTER
Thirteen

FORGIVENESS | MY PERSONAL STORY

SHATTERED BUT NOT DESTROYED

Dear Journal

> "
>
> So many questions and no answers.
>
> "

Francesca

13 Chapter
FORGIVENESS | MY PERSONAL STORY

Forgiveness is one of the hardest things a person can ever do. Nothing prepared me for the challenge of forgiving the person who murdered my daughter, Francesca. In the aftermath of her death, I wrestled with feelings of anger, betrayal, and an overwhelming sense of loss. I felt as though I had every right not to forgive the person who had inflicted such immeasurable pain on my family, in fact, it felt natural to harbor resentment and to dislike him, even though I didn't know who he was. How could I be expected to forgive someone who not only took my daughter's life, but also left a wound so deep that it continues to shape every aspect of my existence?

The emotions I felt were valid. As a mother, the anger was justified. Losing Francesca to violence was the ultimate betrayal. I believe that if I held onto my anger, I could keep her memory alive in a way that honors the depth of the injustice done to her. There was a part of me that feared forgiving her murderer would be like condoning the act, diminishing the significance of what happened. After all, forgiveness often feels like a release, a letting go. But how could I let go of something so painful tied to my love for Francesca?

For a long time, I resisted the idea of forgiving. In many ways it felt like I was betraying her by even entertaining the thought. The anger became a companion, a reminder of what had been taken from me. It felt like I was protecting her memory by holding on to my right not to forgive, and I was certain that God would understand my reasoning. After all, the magnitude of the crime was not just any ordinary offense, it was murder, the ultimate act of cruelty. Surely, God would not expect me to extend grace where there seemed to be none deserved.

As time went on, however, I began to understand that this anger, though justified, was not serving me or Francesca's memory and the way I thought it was. The weight of carrying it was unbearable. I realized that the unforgiveness was consuming me slowly, taking away pieces of me, too. It wasn't until I confronted these feelings that I began to see how forgiveness is not about excusing the act or forgetting the pain. It's about releasing myself from the grip, the hate and resentment I had in my heart.

The journey toward forgiveness didn't happen overnight and I didn't rush it, but I begin to understand that forgiveness was more about freeing my soul and honoring Francesca's memory in a way that allowed me to live again. Even in her absence, it was about finding peace in a situation where there was none and releasing the anger so that I could continue moving forward with my life and her memory.

Forgiveness is the act of letting go of resentment, anger or the desire for revenge toward someone who has wronged or hurt you. It's a conscious decision to release negative feelings, even if the other person doesn't deserve it or ask for it. Forgiving doesn't mean that you are condoning or excusing the wrong done to you, but it's a personal choice to free yourself from bitterness and allow healing to take place in your heart. Forgiveness wasn't just for the person who caused the harm, but for me. Forgiveness is not a one-time event. It is a journey.

To every woman reading this: From my heart to your heart, I want you to know that yes, your pain is real, but so is your strength. You may feel broken, lost or overwhelmed, but there is a purpose in your life that goes far beyond the hardships you've faced. You're not defined by what has happened to you but how you rise in the midst of it. No matter how dark your days may feel you have a light within you that no one can extinguish. I want you to know that you are worthy of love, respect and happiness. You are worthy of peace and healing. Whatever your story is, whatever you carry, physical, emotional or mental scars, none of them disqualify you from receiving love, or of being able to dream again. Your past does not determine your future.

There is a wealth of hidden treasure inside you, containing all the tools you need to overcome every obstacle—qualities and strengths you haven't yet used, but which are not visible on the surface. These hidden tools are often revealed during trials. When the weight of grief, abuse, or loss feels unbearable, remember that you are not alone. God sees you. He knows your pain, and He stands with you, offering His unshakable love. His promise to you is this: He will never leave you nor forsake you, He is with you until the end. You are loved, you are seen, and you are never forgotten. Cry if you must. Shout if you must. But do not let your heart give up. There is hope for you, a life full of meaning and purpose still ahead of you. You are a survivor, and every step forward you are creating a new path for yourself. Believe in that strength. Believe in the love that surrounds you. And know that, just as *Cry Loud, Spare Not, Speak Up, Inc.* was born out of Francesca's story, your story, too, can bring light, healing and hope to others.

You are not alone in this journey. You are a woman of worth, a woman of resilience, compassion, intuition, courage, empathy, perseverance, patience, love and faith. You are God's masterpiece, and the world is better because YOU are in it.

CHAPTER
Fourteen

DEAR YOU

SHATTERED BUT NOT DESTROYED

Dear Journal

"

"Love Letter"

I love you simply
Your eyes your smile
Your mind body and soul
When you're just waking up in
the morning
When your hair is a mess
When your skin is ashy
When your eyes are heavy
from stress
When you didn't get your nails
done
When your eyebrows touch
I love you simply.
I love ME!

"

Francesca

14 *Chapter*
DEAR YOU

TO THE MURDERER: Dear whoever you are, I think I'll call you, Dear you...

Dear You,

Even though I don't know you, in a weird sort of way, you have become an uninvited part of my life. Today, I prayed for you. I committed you to God, asked him to take you out of my thoughts and to heal all my uncertainties and emotions tied to you. To break all ungodly soul ties that may have come through the grief and pain over the loss of my daughter's life and the life of her unborn son, they were brutally murdered from your hands.

I pray I can get through writing this letter to you. My emotions are getting the best of me. It's the loss of a child, It's a mother's cry. It's a cry that never seems to stop. Even when I'm not crying on the outside, my heart continuously cries on the inside. If you put my heart under a microscope, you will find its broken into a million pieces. There's no ending to the pain. Even though you took my daughter's life, I wouldn't want your mother or father to experience the pain, the sadness, the grief we are dealing with.

Let me introduce myself, I am Francesca Harris-Scarborough's (the victim's) mother and her deceased son's grandmother. My grandson will never get to know me, and I will never get to know him. Even though he was a few months old in the womb, he was murdered too.

Sometimes I wonder if you know me, if you know my family. Have we met? Do you ever think how this tragedy has affected our family, how it has affected me?

I get mad at me for giving you the credit of having a heart, to think that anything would affect you after the way you murdered my daughter and grandson.

Tell me about you, do you have family, child, or children, mother, father, siblings, spouse, girlfriend? It must be nice if you answered yes to be able to see, touch, hug, talk to them, to celebrate with them, their victories. To be able to honor your parents. Francesca, I call her Franny had a birthday in November and I couldn't eat with her, celebrate her, do the things that you have the privilege of doing with your family on special days or on a daily basis.

The pain you have caused me is unreal, there were times I didn't know what the day would hold, to get out of the bed was a chore, to go to work was the hardest thing. I couldn't focus. I would write down what I needed to do and applaud myself if I accomplished one thing. There were days and nights I would cry for hours. I couldn't go to family functions or be around anyone. I want you to understand the effect of your actions. What makes you so special that you don't have to give answers or have consequences? My life has completely changed. I now understand the man or woman that stands on the street, the man or woman suffering from addictions, the man or woman that gave up on life, or that struggles with mental illness/depression. I have no judgments now, because if it had not been for the Lord on my side, I would have fainted, given up or even attempted to retaliate. I am glad I have a relationship with Him. This is one thing I couldn't do on my own. The pain is unbearable. Even as I write this, I'm feeling the pain but grateful to God for allowing me not to have a story of defeat.

Today has been a very rough day, it's been raining all morning. Rainy and gloomy days are hard for me, I know Francesca is not there, her spirit is with the Lord. The mother in me can't help but think of her in that cold, cruel ground. I feel so robbed, so cheated. I have gone through many things in my life, but this one is the hardest. Tell me, was killing her the only alternative for you? The first year of her death I checked on her almost every day at the cemetery. I had to come to reality that this was her new address. I had to make sure she was ok. The pain level in my heart is so excruciating I know only God can heal it. I believe he's allowing this pain because His purpose will prevail.

I feel as though my words are competing with my heart and my faith. I feel like Job, "though you slay me yet will I trust you, Lord." I don't understand the who, what, when, where and how's that happening in my life but one thing we can both know is that God is in the midst, he does not slumber or sleep, He sees everything. Every detail of our script, our life.

There are days my eyes hurt and burn from the tears. I believe the tears and my heart are attached because some tears are silent, and my heart is tired.

I have to tell you, Dear you, you have truly caused chaos and trauma in my life and in my body. It seems as though everything has a connection to Francesca. I cry when there is a marriage because it will never happen for her, I cry at the birthdays of babies because I'll never get to know her child, I cry on Mother's Day, I look at her dad and cry for him on Father's Day because he has to always be my strength and can't let go the way I do. I cry when I see the pain and grief my family is experiencing. The sadness in their eyes. I cry because we have to pick our time to talk about her and when we do, she is the *Late* Francesca. I cried on my anniversary because I was asked how many children we have; I didn't know whether to say three or two. When asked, how many grandchildren I have, I relive everything that happened.

Dear you, have you ever seen your mother and your father cry? How do you feel when you see them cry? No one wants to see their parents' cry. Do they know that you did this dreadful, horrific crime?

I cry when I say her name, see her picture, see anything that is connected to her. I cried because I wasn't there to protect her.

Dear you, did you realize that April 8, 2024 will be four years that Francesca was brutally murdered. I guess that was a dumb question, of course you did. My heart is soooooo broken. I didn't know that I housed so many tears, I was a person that didn't cry, but you changed that. Some parents will be celebrating a child's birthday on that day, But I will be remembering her death date. I will be remembering the morning sitting at my desk receiving a call to meet the detectives and to hear the news that my daughter was found dead in her car on Blakely Street. What was important about that street, that spot? How did you get her there? Did she know that you were taking her there and why did she think she was going there? I cry about the horrific way she died. You shot her two times in the heart. Did you want to make sure that she died? Do you have a child, sister? Stop and think of how you would feel if someone did that to them. Would you be able to be silent, sit and do nothing as I / my family have done?

If you're the father of her child, do you stop and think of the baby? Do you grieve about the baby? How do you feel when you're around other children, knowing that you killed your child? If the baby had lived, he would have been a boy. A father is supposed to protect not hurt.

What happened in your childhood? Someone must have really rejected you, hurt you, disappointed you, violated you. My feelings towards you have been frozen, but I'm feeling sorry for you, I am crying in my spirit for you Franny was very tiny and timid, her voice was timid, she wouldn't hurt a fly. She stayed to herself. She was smart, gifted, and beautiful.

I have so many unresolved questions that continuously flood my mind. The first one being the obvious, why did you kill her?

Did you plan her murder? She was killed in such a cold-blooded manner. I believe I would have mourned her death differently if she had been sick, I could even accept a car accident. How did you meet Francesca? Were you her lover? Why did you shoot her two times in the heart? Why did you shoot her at all? Were you serious about your relationship with her, and what was that relationship?

Did she suffer a lot? Did she die quickly? Did you torture her? I hope she died in a quick manner and did not suffer.

Did she see the gun? Did she have a conversation with you before it happened, or did you ambush her? What were her last words?

Was she trying to protect her unborn child? Did she beg for her life?

Do you ever think of what you have done? Are you even sorry? Did you cry? Franny was my baby. She was my daughter. Did you gain the self-satisfaction that you were seeking or needed? She was left murdered in her car from 9 PM to 7 AM. How could you leave her like that? Stray animals are treated better than that. What did you do after you killed her, after you left the crime? Did you go to eat, did you get high, did you celebrate, go to bed? Were you alone when you killed her? Were you hired to kill her? What did you have to gain? Did she mean anything to you? Did you know that she was pregnant?

If you have a child or children, did you go home and check on your child's well-being after you killed your unborn child? I need you to stop and look at that child or children now, would you take their life? Are they safe in your presence?

Did you smell the gunpowder on your hand, look at your fingers? Are you that cold? I asked you earlier what happened to you in your childhood? It had to be something that happened to you to make you heartless and selfish. Do you think you're heartless, selfish or is killing the norm for you? Have you killed before?

As I'm writing this letter, my heart is thawing out. Other than anger, I didn't know what I felt concerning you. I know that I couldn't hate you because I have the love of God in my heart and God is love. But I couldn't feel love for you either, my heart has been numbed. I now find myself crying for you, for your family. I really feel sorry for you. I'm crying because she chose a friend, lover, associate, like you. I'm crying for your children, grandchildren, their grandchildren, generations to come that will feel the effect of your SIN. You think you have gotten away, but one or more generations will feel the effect of your action and your hard heart.

I feel sorry for you, because it's something to have to live life with bloody hands from the shedding of innocent blood. Take a look at your hands, blood covered. When you look in the mirror, who do you see? Do you see the man of the hour, the big man on campus, man that got by, or do you see a wimp, a coward, a narcissist. I need you to tell me what or who do you see? Do you see greed, money, tell me what do you see? Do you see remorse, do you see sorrow?

Dear you, it has to be so hard being you, your label is a MURDERER, actually a DOUBLE MURDERER. Having that in your mind and heart 24 hours a day must be a heavy load to carry. No peace, just merely pretending and existing.

Dear you, you might be walking around looking free, you may wear the finest clothes, you may drive the best vehicle, your pockets may be loaded with money but you are bound, chained, gagged, your body is feeling the effect of the pain you caused and is causing my family, Your mind is holding you hostage, as you read this I guaranteed you that you relived the experience. No one is above the physical law, you think you have gotten away, but you will always be there, you can't run from you. Every time you look in the mirror, you have to deal with yourself. If you hide in a corner, you will have to face you, where you go, whatever you do you will have to deal with you. We will always reap what we have sown. You can't hide from you, your heart won't let you, every time you look in the mirror, you will see that night, you will see her blood in your mind, when the room gets quiet, in the dark of the night you will hear her scream.

Does your mind play tricks on you? Do you look in the mirror to see yourself and she's looking at you? I believe you see it now as you read this letter. Was she a threat to you in any way? Did she have something on you?

Dear you, I asked God to not let hatred, bitterness, retaliation take root in my heart, to have peace in knowing that vengeance was His to repay. I asked him to give me the strength to not let me hate you, to forgive you.

Dear you, did you know that Jesus died on the cross for your sins and my sins, that He shed his blood for the remission of our sins? Did you know that he rose on the third day so that you may have life and have it more abundantly.

Ask God for mercy. God is a forgiving God. He forgave us for our sins because He already knew that we would commit them. On the cross Jesus asked the Father to forgive you and me because we know not what we are doing. The Lord told me that Francesca's death would be used for His glory. Francesca's death will not be in vain. God is replacing beauty for ashes and her memory will used for women to live and be healed.

Have you asked for forgiveness? Ask God to forgive you. If you confess your sins, He is faithful and just to forgive you and cleanse you from all unrighteousness. When you receive His forgiveness, you will have no problem writing me a letter back with answers, details, giving me the closure I so desire. My email is cryloudsparenotspeakup.com.

Dear you, for the young girl that does not know her worth, I forgive you. For the young lady that is in an abusive relationship that needs to get out, I forgive you. For the lady that thinks the only way she is loved is to be abused, I forgive you. For the lady that thinks she is at fault and that she deserved the abuse, I forgive you. For the lady who lost a child due to abuse, I forgive you.

For every girl, every young lady that is waiting for healing, waiting to be set free, I forgive you.

I forgive you for murdering my daughter, Francesca Monet Harris-Scarborough. I forgive you. I forgive you for murdering my unborn Grandson. I forgive you for the hurt, pain, chaos, for the disruption, you have caused me.

I forgive you. Death can't hold Franny in the ground, she will rise again, through each of these women, through each of their testimonies she will rise. Your purpose was not completed, you tried to kill her to shut her up, but her spirit will never die. You will see her in books, movies, newspapers, and social media. You will see her in your house, when you look at your wife, you will see her unborn son through your son, your grandson. She will rise, and my healing will come through each lady that overcomes abuse, each lady that survives abuse and the mothers that won't have to live the nightmare and feel the pain I felt and continue to feel.

Dear you, I gently place you in the hands of our Lord. The peace that I have through this grief and pain is that Francesca may be gone but she will never be forgotten. Through her memory many lives will be saved. Her tiny voice will sound like a trumpet. Through her memory she will be heard and seen more than when she was physically alive. Francesca will live in the hearts of many, many, women. Today, I will visit her grave and put flowers on it with a new perspective. A heart of forgiveness. Thank you, Lord.

Justice has prevailed.

FORGIVENESS LIST

MAKE A LIST OF THOSE YOU NEED TO FORGIVE

♡ _____

♡ _____

♡ _____

♡ _____

♡ _____

♡ _____

♡ _____

♡ _____

*For if you forgive other people when they sin against you, your heavenly Father will also
forgive you. But if you do not forgive others their sins, your Father will not forgive your sins
Matthew 6:14-15 [NIV]*

RESOURCES

Listed below are a few resources that may be useful to you. **We do not endorse or guarantee that either agency listed below are right for you.** We understand that seeking assistance is very scary and can be dangerous based on your situation. Please be advised that when seeking assistance on digital products such as computers and/or cell phones, your abuser may be able to recover your search history. Clear your browser and seek assistance with deleting your digital footprint. Be careful.

Domestic Violence Resources

National Domestic Abuse Hotline: thehotline.org
Confidential Support: 24/7/365

The National Domestic Abuse Hotline provides information on shelters and non-shelter providers, a toll-free hotline number (1-800-799-7233), you can chat live at any time, and/or text "START" to 88788 (messaging and data rates may apply) to speak to a counselor or representative.

Other Organizations

- Womenshealth.gov
- Nationalwomensshelternetwork.org
- Domesticshelters.org
- Victimconnect.org

Grief Resources

We highly encourage you to seek professional counseling to assist you with the grief that you are dealing with. Grief is different for everyone; therefore, you need someone that understands your pain. There are also groups such as *griefshare.org* or the *compassionatefriends.org* in which you can look for a grief group in your area. You may find different resources in your area. I can't stress enough, seek help.

Suicide Prevention

I can understand the pain that you are in and all the thoughts that may be running through your mind. One of those thoughts may be suicide, but I tell you right now, that is **NOT** the answer. As you have read in my book, turn this pain into power. Honor your loved one by helping someone else when you are mentally and physically strong enough. Focus on the scriptures and affirmations that I have provided and above all, seek HELP with a professional counselor in your area. If you are unable to talk to a counselor, call the 24/7/365 national suicide prevention hotline at 800-273-8255 or just dial 988. The National Suicide Hotline Designation Act designated 988 as the national number to call for suicide prevention. Please do so immediately.

MEET THE
AUTHOR ♥
Shirley H. Scarborough

Born on October 12, 1959, in Elmont, Virginia, Shirley is a beacon of faith, resilience, and love. The 11th of 17 siblings, she graduated from the Hanover County Public School System and studied Early Childhood Development at J. Sargeant Reynolds Community College. For over 44 years, she has been married to her loving husband, Robert Scarborough Jr., and together they've raised their children: Pastor Robert Scarborough III, LaShara Foster, the late Francesca Harris-Scarborough, and son-in-love Arek Foster Sr. Shirley is also a proud grandmother to Sa'Riyah, Ka'mari, and AJ.

Shirley answered the call to ministry in 1998 as an Evangelist and has served faithfully at The Word Church International Ministries for over 18 years, leading the Women's Fellowship under her son's pastorship. Known for her compassionate heart and prayerful spirit, she has dedicated her life to supporting women, families, and marriages.

Her passion for children led her to co-found Signs and Wonders Daycare/Learning Center LLC in 1998, a state-licensed childcare center that has thrived for over 26 years. Her love for crafting led her to establish Stitches of Love, creating handmade gifts and floral arrangements in memory of her late mother.

In 2020, Shirley faced unimaginable grief when her daughter Francesca and her unborn grandchild were tragically taken from her. Determined to turn her pain into purpose, Shirley founded *Cry Loud, Spare Not, Speak Up, Inc.*, a 501(c)(3) nonprofit organization dedicated to empowering women affected by domestic violence and abuse. This initiative provides education, support, and resources, encouraging women to break the silence, reclaim their voices, and recognize their worth. Each year, near the anniversary of Francesca's death, Shirley hosts the "I Am Enough, I Know My Worth," conference, which inspires women and girls, aged 12 and older, to embrace self-esteem and empowerment.

Shirley's commitment and impact have garnered widespread recognition. She has been featured in the Richmond Free Press as "Personality of the Week," interviewed by CBS 6, and highlighted in Bold Journey Magazine. In 2024, she was honored as a Hometown Hero for her tireless dedication to her faith, family, and community.

Through every triumph and challenge, Shirley H. Scarborough's life is a testament to her faith in God, boundless compassion, and unwavering resilience. Her story continues to inspire others to find strength, healing, and purpose in the face of adversity.

Correspondences |
To write to the author, please send an email to:
authorshirleyscarborough@gmail.com

Please include your testimony or how this book has blessed your life or a loved one. Your prayer requests are welcome.

Join Us |
Want to join our movement of *Cry Loud, Spare Not, Speak Up, Inc.*, please contact us and we would love to see you at our next conference or hear your story.

Speaking Engagements |
I would love to visit your conference, organization, and/or church to shout to the world how God turned my pain into purpose. Please contact me. I look forward to meeting you in person.

Social Media |
Follow us on the following platforms:
YouTube: @CryLoudSpeakUp
IG: @AuthorShirleyScarborough
TT: @author_shirley.s
FB: Cry Loud, Spare not, Speak Up

URGENT PLEA

Thank you for reading my book and extending your prayers to me and my family. I pray that this book changes your life, and you turn your pain into purpose.

Your feedback is vital to the success of this book and the spread of hope and healing whether you experienced the grief of a loved one or you have a powerful testimony of escaping a domestic violence situation. There is no judgement here. Let me know your story because it could bless someone else.

Please take two minutes to leave me a helpful review along with your kind words on Amazon.

PUBLISHING
CEO Publishing
715 E 4th Street, Studio 2 | Richmond, VA 23224
ceopublishingeditors@gmail.com
www.ceopublishingllc.com

COACHING/COVER DESIGNER
Danielle Harris-Branch
www.daniellehbranch.com

EDITOR
Roderick K. Thomas
Lions Pride Productions

FORMAT, DESIGN & ILLUSTRATION
Alonda West-Johnson
LaLovely Photography
infinitelalovely@gmail.com
www.lalovelyphotography.com

PHOTOGRAPHY
Orrie Gaines

AUTHOR ASSISTANT
Tivoli Dabney

QR CODE VOICES
Author Shirley Scarborough
Tivoli Dabney as the voice of Francesca Harris-Scarborough

BIBLICAL REFERENCES

Holy Bible, Evangelical Heritage Version. Milwaukee: Northwestern Publishing House, 2019. 2 Corinthians 1:8.

Holy Bible, New International Version®, NIV® Copyright © 1973, 1978, 1984, 2011 by Biblica, Inc.® Used by permission. All rights reserved.

Holy Bible, New Living Translation, Copyright © 1996, 2004, 2015 by Tyndale House Foundation. Used by permission of Tyndale House Publishers, Inc., Carol Stream, Illinois 60188. All rights reserved.

Scriptures noted KJV are taken from the King James Version of the Bible.

MUSICAL REFERENCE

Britten, Graham, and Terry Britten. *What's Love Got to Do with It.* Performed by Tina Turner. Capitol Records, 1984.